OVERCOME BULLYING
FOR PARENTS

ACKNOWLEDGEMENTS

Many of the suggestions in this book are based on the ideas of Parent Network, the national charity that provides parenting education programmes.

Acknowledgement is also due to Kidscape, the charity dedicated to children's safety; to the Anti-Bullying Campaign; and to Lorraine Demko, Senior Health Promotion Adviser of Eastern Surrey Health Promotion, for being a source of inspiration and authority on the 'No-blame' approach to bullying.

Grateful thanks to Alan Craig, Paul Appleby and Tim Jones for technical support, to Lyn Castle for offering space in her home as a writing retreat, to friends, family and colleagues for encouragement, and to all those who have shared their pain, their learnings and their stories so that others may learn from them.

S.R.M.

OVERCOME BULLYING
FOR PARENTS

Sheila Munro

Piccadilly Press • London

Photoset from author's disk by Zena Flax.
Printed and bound by WBC, Bridgend
for the publishers Piccadilly Press Ltd.,
5 Castle Road, London NW1 8PR

A catalogue record for this book is available from
the British Library

ISBN: 1 85340 490 X

Other books in the How To Help Your Child series:
SPELLING FOR PARENTS
GRAMMAR FOR PARENTS
READING FOR PARENTS
MATHS FOR PARENTS
INFORMATION TECHNOLOGY FOR PARENTS
WRITING FOR PARENTS
CHILD SAFETY FOR PARENTS

Cover design by Paul Cooper Design

Sheila Munro is a journalist, trainer and communication consultant. She has worked in the field of parent support and education for six years, and has written and broadcast extensively on parenting issues, including bullying. She spent many years working in community education and has a Certificate in Adult and Continuing Education from the University of Nottingham. She was born in Glasgow, lives in London and is the parent of a teenage son.

CONTENTS

FOREWORD

It is quite likely that you are reading this book because you're worried about your child being bullied, or that he or she may be a bully. The consequences of bullying are now well-known: as well as physical damage, the mental and emotional scars can be borne into adulthood. Newspapers report cases of adults seeking damages from former schools, associating bullying with their under-achievement at school. Schools have a responsibility to provide education for children in a safe learning environment, but that, unfortunately, is not always the reality...

Bullying can cause untold distress to both parents and children. And yet, until recently, it was almost as big a taboo as child abuse: you didn't talk about it and, if a child complained about it to an adult, he or she was seen as 'wimpish'. ('Go out and fight them, sonny!')

Fortunately, attitudes are changing, and bullying is being recognised as abuse. However, it is still rife, not just in schools but throughout our society, and the aim of this book is to help parents (and carers) deal with the whole difficult subject, from talking about it with their children to taking appropriate action. It also offers skills and strategies for parents to help their children feel more equipped to deal with, and prevent bullying. Please note, different things work for different people and there is no guarantee that the strategies I've included are going to work for you.

Finally, it suggests some longer term solutions.

Chapter One

DEFINING THE PROBLEM

Bullying has been around for a long time and is deeply rooted in our culture. It causes mental and emotional pain as well as physical injury. It can be almost as distressing to parents as it is to children. As a parent or carer, you may be concerned about your child being bullied, or about the possibility that she or he is being a bully. You may have painful memories of bullying incidents from your own school days.

Before attempting to take the bull by the horns, so to speak, and overcome it (with apologies to the bull!), it is important to form a clear picture of what bullying is and to have an understanding of the many issues involved. This will help not only in handling what needs to be handled but also in taking preventative measures.

WHAT IS BULLYING?

What exactly do we mean by bullying? Bullying is not just physical attack; it can also be verbal, emotional or psychological, or all of these together. It may be very obvious and shocking – for witnesses as well as victim – or it may be covert, silent and invisible, with neither adult nor other children even being aware that it is going on, let alone the effect it might be having on a child.

Some experts consider aggression as bullying only if the bullying behaviour continues over a period of time, rather than being a one-off act of aggression. Others believe that even one-off acts of aggression can constitute a severe episode of bullying that could affect someone for the rest of their life.

DIFFERENT KINDS OF BULLYING

(i) Physical
Physical bullying can include hitting, kicking, punching, scratching or biting.

Stevie: "It all got too much for me, the constant prodding and poking, the quick nudge, the dig with the elbow, the sharp kick – all sly things that other people – teachers and pupils – didn't see... it wore me down completely."

(ii) Psychological
Pyschological bullying can mean excluding someone, 'sending them to Coventry' – not speaking to them.

Helen: "I went to a Convent school. The girls in my class used to turn their back on me. I didn't know what was going on but now I know it was a form of bullying. It went on for years..."

It could also be extortion, threats, damage to personal property or spreading nasty rumours or mocking or ridiculing someone.

(iii) Verbal

Teasing can be bullying: not just a playful remark (though even so-called 'playful' remarks can cause much pain) but relentless tormenting or name-calling, of a personal or sexist or racist nature.

Irma: "I simply couldn't bear it, the bantering, tormenting, psychological and verbal abuse. It made me ill..."

Sexual harrassment (which can be verbal, physical and psychological), whilst not bullying is also totally unacceptable.

BULLYING AND IMBALANCE OF POWER

A key component of all types of bullying is the use of intimidation as power. There is a power imbalance between bully and victim, either in strength – for example, where a larger (and possibly older) child picks on a smaller (possibly younger) or weaker child – or in numbers, where a group picks on an individual. A quarrel between friends or the occasional fight between equals is not considered bullying.

Sometimes the power imbalance is emotional or psychological. Some people who bully have powerful psyches and sometimes it is easy to feel overpowered by them, especially at times of feeling weak or vulnerable. In a recent survey, bullies were found to have very good management potential because they understood people's psyches and had excellent skills in manipulation! This challenges the stereotype of the bully as a mindless thug. (It also puts into question qualities of management!)

Jim: "I wasn't your average picture of bullying, picking on kids. I never crept up on kids. Didn't target them. But being school 'policemen', some kids we would slap about. I was always a fighter, but I didn't think of it as bullying."

The other side of the coin, of course, is that many bullies whose anti-social behaviour goes unchecked as children, end up with criminal convictions as adults, their patterns of aggression and intimidation having become more and more entrenched.

WHO BULLIES?

Girls are as capable as boys of bullying, including physical bullying, though traditionally bullying by girls has been seen as taking a more covert, manipulative form. The most common form of bullying in schools takes place by pupils in the same class or the same year, although it can be done by younger as well as older children. Bullies come in many shapes and sizes.

DISCUSSING BULLYING WITH YOUR CHILD

It might help you and your child if you discuss together your understanding of what bullying behaviour is. (Do this at a time when you are both calm and collected: not at times of crisis!) Perhaps relate it to a story or a news item – a situation where neither of you is directly involved. Raising awareness in this way and giving the problem a name makes it easier for your child (and you!) to talk about it should a problem arise.

George: "Sam had a bit of a stutter. We knew he was

teased about it, but he was quite a good-natured child and we didn't realise how badly the teasing had affected him. Not until a couple of years later, that is, when he'd changed schools and felt able to talk about it for the first time. Apparently he'd felt suicidal... I feel so bad that ı didn't do anything about it, but I had no idea. It's only now, putting a name to it, that we recognise he was being bullied."

Of course, there are different degrees of bullying, from mild to extreme. But remember, every individual experiences a situation differently. What might seem 'mild' to an onlooker may have had a devastating effect on the recipient. Or what might appear extremely rough and aggressive may leave a person relatively unscathed. Different personalities, different children react in different ways.

Sometimes a child may not realise she or he is bullying – if teasing, for example, she/he might not realise the effect it is having on the person being teased. She or he might be shocked to realise they're hurting someone. In these cases, having a firm and gentle word with your child might be all that's needed to 'nip' bullying in the bud. The earlier children are made aware of this, the better.

WHERE BULLYING TAKES PLACE

Bullying can happen anywhere. The culture of bullying doesn't exist only in schools! It permeates all stratas of society, from the home (including domestic violence) to the shop-floor to public services to Parliament. In a survey carried out by the Institute of Personnel and Development, one in eight people reported being bullied in the workplace in the last five years. This included managers and professional staff being bullied.

Teachers, feeling bullied by managers or other staff, are more likely to feel miserable and to pass on a culture of bullying to the children. Unfortunately, teachers have been known to be bullied by parents as well. We are all in this together! Remember, many teachers are parents too.

Fortunately, although the picture may still seem bleak, there is a growing movement to overcome bullying. More and more people are speaking out about their experiences and many positive initiatives are going on in communities and schools, with significant results. There are also more avenues of support for children, including counselling services and helplines.

Stevie: "I wish they'd had Childline when I was younger; it might have helped me. Maybe if Parentline had existed then it would have helped my father..."

In schools, research shows there is a higher incidence of bullying in secondary schools but it is worryingly prevalent in primary schools as well. It can occur in any kind of school, from boys' schools to girls' schools to co-educational; from public, boarding schools to day comprehensives, from totally independent schools to country village primaries.

In school, bullying can happen in the playground, the classroom or the corridors. It can happen in the toilets or unsupervised outside areas (especially when children are older and know that such behaviour is not allowed).

As well as happening at school, bullying can happen on the journey to or from school.

Kate (teacher): "There's a girl hiding in the toilets right now, too petrified to go home."

and:

Stevie: "I got used to running home every day from school. I used to escape through the old railway next to the school, which ran past the school and past the allotments next to our house. It became my escape route, and because I spent so much time there I got to know all the nooks and crannies, the best bushes to hide in."

and:

Doug: "I used to get bullied on the way to school by pupils from another school. I walked to school with the fear of being bullied and arrived at school in a state of fear, which seemed to attract more bullying... Then I would be afraid to walk home again. So, I walked about a mile in detour and learned evasive strategies, the biggest of which was not to go to school! I would spend all day in the woods on my own. Although I did have a fear of being on my own, and of being found out, that was preferable to the fear of being bullied."

(Note: These case studies are intended not to alarm but to keep us alert to dangers.)

One of the effects of bullying is that it can lead to truancy. Later in this chapter we will look at the emotional and long-term effects of bullying.

SYMPTOMS OF BULLYING

A child being bullied may be in an anxious or agitated state. She or he may seem afraid to go to school, or come home from school with torn clothes or personal possessions missing or schoolbooks damaged. She or he may be ravenous from missing lunch, having had dinner money stolen. There may be unexplained injuries – for example, bruises or cuts – or the child might be uncharacteristically withdrawn.

There might be signs of school work suddenly deteriorating or of regressive behaviour, such as bedwetting.

If your child displays one or more of these symptoms, there is a chance she or he may be being bullied or intimidated. However, resist jumping to conclusions! Alarming though it may be, there may be other reasons for the behaviour. For example, it is quite normal for children (and adults!) to regress in behaviour from time to time, though this happens in different ways for different people!

DENIAL

One of the biggest problems about bullying is the secrecy and denial which surrounds it. Like other forms of abuse, it holds the threat of 'don't tell anyone or else...' thus perpetuating feelings of fear – and sometimes terror – along with the inevitable pain.

(i) Denial by Children

Children are afraid to tell the teacher in case they or their friends are bullied even more. Or they're afraid to tell their parents in case their parent tells the teacher. They may even be ashamed to tell their parents, feeling they've 'let them down' in some way, that being bullied is a sign of 'weakness'. They could even be protecting their parents, as in Jim's case:

"I already knew they couldn't handle it..."

Feelings of fear can spiral down into feelings of hopelessness.

Irma: "I gave up. No one seemed bothered, or even to notice. Nobody wanted to help me."

Children may be desperate for an adult to intervene but feel unable to ask for help. So much is the pressure not to tell, that often children will deny that anything is wrong even if they are asked by a caring parent or teacher.

(ii) Denial by Teachers

Bullying is sometimes ignored by teachers, often because they have not detected it, or, they might know that 'something' is going on but not the extent to which it is happening, or the effect it is having on the victim.

Or, they may feel powerless to act unless the bullying is physical:

Molly: "Sharon (a teenager) had been threatened with her life – they said 'you know so-and-so who was knived: well, that could happen to you.' We only found this out when she blurted it out between bouts of being sick at the hospital, after taking an overdose. When she was better we went up to the school to talk to the teachers. They called in one of the gang but later said they couldn't do anything – it would have been better, they said, if she (the gang member) had hit Sharon, 'then we could have done something'!"

Sometimes, if a child has plucked up the courage to tell and the parents then go to the school to confront the teacher, the teacher denies that any bullying is going on. Or they might say the child's imagining it or 'exaggerating'.

One father, Biri, took matters into his own hands:

"They said there was nothing wrong but I knew something was up. So I went and spied on them in the playground one day! Then I saw what was going on. The older boys took his lunch money. They'd been doing that every day. No wonder he was so angry and moody when he came home from school – he hadn't been eating all day."

Another parent, Donna, encountered a similar 'playing-down' of what was happening with her son:

'They're bound to get bumps, knocks and bruises in the rough and tumble of school life. But thirty bruises? That's how many there were on his stomach and back – I counted them. Strictly from football? That's what his teacher said. And if that were the case, they shouldn't be allowed to 'play' so roughly..."

Donna's son also had problems with children jumping on him from behind:

"As well as being downright dangerous, causing him nasty injuries when he fell to the ground, it made him feel shocked and powerless: being jumped on you're caught unawares, unprepared for it. The teacher thought it was 'just a game the children were playing in the playground'."

Understandably, some teachers prefer to 'turn a blind eye' rather than have to deal with bullying. They may not know how to handle it. Or, they may already be working in an impossibly pressurised situation.

Many teachers feel frustrated because they know that dealing with one incident will not solve the problem of bullying in the school without the support of their Head or other staff or the back-up of an effective anti-bullying policy.

Some schools are loathe to admit they have a bullying problem because they're afraid it may damage their reputation, even though having an anti-bullying policy would surely enhance it. Nowadays, in a culture of 'parental choice', some schools worry that admitting to any problem will make the school unpopular.

(iii) Denial by Parents

Many adults still consider bullying as an almost inevitable part of 'growing up' (a belief held especially amongst men), and that 'telling tales' is a sign of weakness. Parents tell their children not to 'make a fuss', in the belief that children have to learn to 'stick up for themselves'. The trouble is that, if they were able to defend themselves against children who were bigger or stronger, they would not have been picked on in the first place!

Often these beliefs stem from messages parents themselves received as children. They may be worried that telling the teacher will mean their children will 'get it in the neck' (from the bullies) or that their child might be punished by the teacher, especially if that was their own experience.

Doug: "After the meeting with my parents and the Headmaster, the bullies were summoned. They were all caned. Then I got caned as well!"

Nowadays, even with the abolition of corporal punishment, schools have sometimes been known to penalise victims. But many schools now have fair and reasonable disciplinary procedures. Don't be put off by your own negative experiences of school.

Parents may feel a sense of shame or failure as a parent that their child is bullied. Or they may feel confused and angry, yet powerless to do anything about it. Often parents can feel very isolated and alone with the problem. Either they don't know who to turn to, or they may not want to go to the school for fear of being seen to 'make a fuss'...

Sometimes parents whose children are bullied find it simpler to ignore the issue than to have to deal with it. Sometimes this is because they have their own deeply buried memories of bullying, and 'switching off' is the subconscious mind's best strategy for not having to deal with one's own pain.

Jim (after being bullied in the park): "I came home in floods of tears. I remember the nanny putting me in the bath. Then she and my mother went out and I could hear them talking outside the room. They said, 'Don't talk about it'. There was a feeling of shame... My parents just weren't equipped to deal with the situation."

And, as a consequence of Jim's parents' denial:

"Next time something happened I didn't tell them because I knew they couldn't deal with it. Maybe, if we had been able to communicate, it would have helped prevent some of the other things that happened."

COLLUSION

Sometimes there is unconscious collusion between a teacher and pupils over bullying. If, for example, a teacher finds a child particularly irritating, he or she may 'allow' a degree of bullying of that child to take place; may, at one level derive satisfaction from the teasing. Or may choose not to intervene:

Stevie, an outsider in a village primary school, was relentlessly bullied by his classmates but the teacher never intervened. "It was only when we had a supply teacher one day (another outsider) that I felt safe to scream and lash out against the people who were attacking me."

Or a teacher may even single out a pupil to mock and ridicule. Sometimes people – even teachers! – may be unaware that they are bullying. But psychologists would say that victimising a child helps the teacher retain or regain control of the class by diverting negative attention away from her/himself and focussing it on someone else. It is very easy for teachers, or any adult with children, to abuse their power and 'rule by fear'. A teacher has the capacity to ridicule, or terrorise a whole class. (Note: let us not forget, it has also been known for teachers to be bullied by a whole class of children...)

Collusion around bullying also takes place between children.

Doug, who went to an all-boys' school, was a victim of 'posting', a brutal initiation 'ceremony' carried out by sixth formers on first formers new to the school, in which the victim was run against a small diameter tree with his legs splayed open, then tied, crosslegged, around the tree with his arms wrapped round the tree as well.

"Then the bell would go and the circle of boys hiding what was happening would disappear, leaving me to get rescued by my friends (then punished by the teacher for being late to

class!) A few years later, when I was one of the bigger boys, I turned a blind eye to what was going on. That saved me from being bullied again. If I'd said anything, I would have been. You were automatically persecuted if you didn't play the game."

LONG-TERM EFFECTS OF BULLYING

Bullying can make children miserable and seriously damage their personal lives as well as their academic performance. Another aspect of the bullying problem has been the tendency to look at bullying as only physical and to deny, or not even be aware of the emotional effect. And yet it is the effect the bullying is having on the victim that is a key factor for the person doing the bullying. It is common for bullies to make the victim feel it is their fault, that they 'deserve' the bullying in some way. Victims often end up feeling ashamed as well as humiliated.

With bullying, comes the constant fear of being bullied. It can make a child feel helpless and inadequate. Possible short-term effects can be mood swings, depression, nightmares, insomnia, all seriously affecting a child's quality of life.

As well as feelings of fear, pain and humiliation, bullying can lead to damaged self-esteem and lack of confidence. It can cause behavioural problems and seriously affect mental and emotional health. Many of the adults quoted in this book are still coming to terms with what happened to them as children. If we can help our children prevent, or overcome bullying issues now, we lessen the possibility of the effects becoming long-term.

Doug: "Because of the bullying, I associated school and learning with pain and fear. I know excitement and fear are two sides of the same coin, but I would have preferred my learning experience to have been one of joy and excitement!"

In the next chapter, we consider some of the causes of bullying: what leads to bullying behaviour and how we can help to prevent it. Before we look at 'bullies', remember that most of us have the capacity to bully, and most of us have been guilty of bullying to a greater or lesser degree at some time in our lives.

Kate: "I don't feel good about it now but it was funny at the time. This boy put too much grease on his hair and we all used to flap our exercise books on his head to get grease marks on the cover. It was a regular occurrence..."

Chapter Two

UNDERSTANDING BULLYING

Jim: "There are many different ways into bullying: psychosis, bizarre ideas, mental thought processes, emotional need..."

Bullying is a complex issue, and the more we understand how and why it happens, the more equipped we are to help prevent it. However, it is vital to stress that, whatever the reasons, or however much understanding there may be, bullying behaviour is unacceptable and always has to be stopped. Tackling the causes may take longer, and brings longer-lasting results.

WHY DO PEOPLE BULLY?

Bullying is a deliberate act intended to cause harm or distress in others. A person who bullies generally does so in order to feel 'big' and powerful, often because inside they may be feeling 'small' and powerless. They may have very low self-esteem. They may bully in order to get attention, as a way of forcing people, almost, to notice them. (These may all be unconscious motives: that is, the things 'driving' the bully's behaviour without her or him necessarily being aware of them.)

Bullying may be a symptom of mental or emotional distress. A person who bullies may be vulnerable, but hates feeling vulnerable, and so attacks others who seem vulnerable instead: almost as a way of attacking his or her own vulnerability. This explains the stereotypical 'tough' bully victimising the sensitive, 'soft' child. Bullying others in order to deny one's own sensitive feelings means that bullying, itself, is a form of denial.

A bully may be someone who has been 'labelled' a bully for so long that the label has stuck and they now identify with that behaviour.

Louise: "I was called a bully at school, and I sure lived up to it... The trouble was, I got the blame for everything. I led a pretty miserable existence, really. Bullies suffer too, you know!"

and:

Jim: "They told me off so often, I decided I'll give them something to tell me off about. I became top rebel."

In Jim's case, the bullying behaviour was a sign that something was wrong. He had been brutalised by the previous headmaster:

"Even when we got a new headmaster, I had already been singled out as a troublemaker. So, I lived up to it."

and:

"Because I had been used to fighting off the abuser, a grown man, for two years, I learned at an early age not to bend over and take it. Fighting became my coping mechanism."

Children who bully may be bullied themselves. They may come from a violent background and only understand the language of aggression. Or they may be joining in with the bullying behaviour or a gang 'just for fun' or for fear of being bullied themselves if they don't.

Children who bully may have family problems. They may be deeply unhappy or insecure. Often bullying, or any disruptive behaviour in children reflects some deep, unmet need.

Pauline (Ashley's mum): "When I used to pick Ashley (aged five) up from school there was another boy, slightly older, who would thump Ashley when they were outside in the playground. I could have wrung his neck! Then one day I found out that the boy had a little brother who had special needs. Then I felt sorry for him. But I wanted the bullying to stop, so I had a chat with his mother. She said, 'Don't worry, he'll be punished, I'll make sure of that.' I'd have much rather seen her put her arms around him and give him some attention. That's probably what he needed more than anything. I think that was the problem. His baby brother was getting all the attention at home. But he couldn't pick on him so he was picking on Ashley instead."

ROLES OF BULLY AND VICTIM

It is important to recognise 'bully' and 'victim' as roles rather than as 'labels' – that is, as a temporary condition and not permanent or fixed. Roles, and behaviour can be changed. There is a danger, if we constantly label a child a 'bully', that she or he may become entrenched in their bullying behaviour. (In the same way that a child labelled 'stupid' starts to act stupid all the time, or a child labelled 'clumsy' becomes even more so! and so on.) It is more helpful think of a child's behaviour as being unacceptable, or difficult, rather than the child her/himself. This gives the child more scope and responsibility to change her or his behaviour, whilst maintaining some self-respect.

Personality factors may also play a part. For example, children who bully may have strong, perhaps over-confident characters, with a 'tough' self-image while those with a tendency to be bullied may feel shy or withdrawn or may be lacking in social skills. This is an over-simplification! The big question is:

THE VICTIM 'ASKED' FOR IT: FACT OR FICTION?

There is a belief, sometimes, that the recipient of bullying behaviour did something to attract the bullying in the first place. That is certainly part of the psychology of bullying, from the bully's point of view, anyway: to make the victim feel that they 'deserve' it. And sometimes victims come to believe that. But generally, victims are mystified as to why they have been picked on in the first place.

Stevie: "Even now, I remember the feeling while I was being held down and beaten: 'WHY ME?' "

People who bully have their own reasons (conscious or unconscious) for targetting someone. It might be 'accidental' in that they need to hurt someone and their 'victim' happens to be in the wrong place at the wrong time, thus making them ideal 'prey', and sometimes setting up a nightmare cycle of hunted and hunter. Or, the most likely scenario, is that they find, or *invent* a specific reason to bully somebody – the reason being something that makes their victim 'different' from them...

But, whatever the differences or the reasons, bullying behaviour is unacceptable.

ATTITUDES THAT GO WITH BULLYING

Up-to-date psychological research shows that the mental processes that accompany bullying and other forms of aggression are an integral *part* of the behaviour, rather than separate from it. It is necessary for someone to perceive someone as 'different' or 'bad' *in order* to bully them. In other words, bullying *begins* as an attitude. Bullying is in the head; physical bullying is just one manifestation of a bullying mind.

A group of people bullying someone may share a common attitude about that person (during the period of bullying, that is). However, attitudes, like behaviour, can change. It is as important to challenge attitudes as the behaviour itself in overcoming bullying. Any kind of prejudice, be it racist, sexist, culturist or ageist contributes towards bullying.

DIFFERENCES

Someone who bullies will find *something*, whether real or imagined, that makes their victim different from them. Sometimes differences reflect social attitudes:

"I was poor, like the others," says Peter, who grew up in

a very poor area, "so I didn't get bullied. But there was a boy who was rich, from a wealthy family but who never spent any money. He got bullied. We all hated him..."

Stevie, from Scotland, was targetted because he was poor:

"They called me 'Scruff' because I came from a poor family who couldn't afford to buy me new clothes."

Differences can be visible. To make things worse for Stevie, he was also the shortest boy in the class. Jo (Donna's son) was the tallest:

"He was the tallest in the class and articulate. It didn't occur to us he would have that sort of problem..."

Lorraine (Jennifer's daughter) had a hairy skin:

"She went to a co-ed school and was teased mercilessly, especially by the boys. It got worse and worse."

Doug was fat and asthmatic, as well as singled out for being brighter, and wanting to ask lots of questions during class. Sometimes a child seems 'different' because she or he doesn't join in games (especially football if he's a boy) or other pursuits:

Eleanor, who was bullied at an all-girls' boarding school, didn't conform: "I felt I had nothing in common with them. I didn't like their pop music, only classical. So I refused to hang out with them in the social room because they were always playing pop."

It was not the first time Eleanor had been made to feel 'different':

"At primary school, some bright spark decided to put me up a year. That's when the bullying started, about age nine. From being invisible, suddenly everyone noticed me! I became the object of hate, the one to be picked on. I was not only the youngest, but the smallest and lightest in the class.

Even before they jumped me up a year I was small; so now I was very, very small."

Children at a new school may be particularly at risk because they are 'outsiders' and without friends at first. Or they may be feeling insecure:

Doug: "When I first started school, maybe it was too early for me to leave home. I don't think I was ready. I was so insecure, I think the bullies smelled it – I got picked on because I had a new school uniform and an older boy wanted my tie. I refused to give it to him so he dragged me round the playground with it, almost strangling me."

Sometimes differences may be in ability or need. Bullies sometimes target children with special needs, although they can also make allowances:

Stevie: "There was another 'scruff' but they never touched him because he had constant operations and was known to be fragile."

Often, however, the differences are more subtle – for example, a child may be singled out who seems slightly withdrawn, or fearful, or displays an inferior or superior air. She or he may come from an over-protective family environment and not be as 'sussed' as other children.

Often the victim doesn't realise she or he is perceived as 'different'! (And no wonder, when it is all in the mind of the bully.) And often, someone who is different doesn't get bullied at all.

Children need to learn that, whatever differences may be apparent, they are just being used as an *excuse* to bully, and that the main reason for bullying behaviour is that the person who bullies feels angry or distressed or unhappy or cruel. Any perceived difference is the *bully's* problem, not the victim's. In some circles, bullying can be a way to try to force a child (or adult) to conform to a code of behaviour or a set of beliefs that is deemed 'normal'. Encourage your child to think for him or herself and to be different if he or she wants to!

SPECIAL NEEDS

Some children may be vulnerable to bullying because of specific problems, such as poor co-ordination, speech or language difficulties, which make them 'different' to other children. In these cases, school staff should be made aware that these pupils may need extra help. Sometimes, preparing all the other children by discussing issues helps to prevent problems.

RESPONDING TO BULLIES

It is an interesting phenomenon that bullying behaviour often depends on the response, to the bullying, by the victim. One of the 'pay-offs' for the bullying mentality is enjoying the fact that the victim suffers. The more distress shown by the victim, the more satisfaction the bully derives. The weaker the victim seems and the less able to defend him or herself, the more the bully feels strong and dominant. How a person responds to teasing, for example, may well influence the bully's decision whether or not to attack in other ways.

There is a recurring refrain, in bullies' descriptions of victims, that they 'didn't stick up for themselves'.

This may seem strange, when they were targetted in the first place for being smaller or unable to defend themselves. But, given the fact that bullying is mental as well as physical, a child may still be able to stand up in non-physical ways to a bully's teasing or tormenting. This can take a lot of inner strength, which we go into in later chapters.

Eleanor: "The whole class picked on me – did things like took my chair away so I had to stand. The teachers? They never seemed to notice. I hadn't been taught by my mother to stick up for myself, I'd been taught to make myself invisible, to disappear. So, it would never have occurred to me to say to the teacher, 'they're picking on me'..."

This went on for a year. Later, at boarding school, Eleanor encountered similar problems:

"It got worse. I still hadn't learned to stick up for myself. Mealtimes were a nightmare. Each 'house' had a dining room. They would bring food to us at the table – cereal or egg or whatever. The rest of the meal was bread and butter and jam. The girls would pass the bread round the table till it got to me and then pass it round the other way, without letting me have any. I nearly starved. I was thirteen by then and growing in inches, but I lost so much weight I came back home a skeleton... That's when Mother thought something was wrong. I was so hungry, every day I spent the whole school day wondering about the next meal. The teachers didn't even notice..."

Bullying behaviour isn't always malicious, however. Sometimes it can be interpreted (mistakenly, perhaps) as a show of strength. In such cases, there may be a code of understanding between bully and victim:

Mike (in the fourth year at boarding school):

"I was hung by my feet out of a third floor window by a guy who was six foot two – a friend! He was a lot bigger than me and showing who was top dog... He had to prove he was bigger and stronger than me (though as far as I was concerned, he didn't have to prove it – I knew!). I wasn't afraid, I trusted him, even though I knew I would die if he let go. I remember looking down at the street below..."

Co-incidentally, Jim (who went to a different school from Mike!) had a similar experience, in reverse:

"I was strong for my age. I remember dangling a kid by his leg out of the window once. This kid was small for his age and I think I was showing my strength. I wasn't going to let go of him..."

Jim also said that showing his strength was a way of not being bullied. He also realised that his need for aggression was not so much to hurt people but:

"...looking for contact, wanting the two-way process, wanting some resistance so you could justify your own aggression."

GROUP DYNAMICS

Sometimes, bullying happens as part of collusion in a group, where people within the group take on different roles. For example, the role of 'scapegoat' is a familiar one. If a child is being made 'scapegoat' at school, she or he may be playing the same role at home. Sometimes, behaviour and roles within a group at school may reflect dynamics within the family. It may be worth asking yourself: does someone in your family consistently play the role of persecutor? Does someone else play victim? Roles, like motives, are usually unconscious, with people being unaware of the roles they and others are playing. However, the more conscious we become of our own, and our child's behaviour, the more able we are to make changes.

Sometimes children adopt a role as a survival strategy. Stevie, who had been a victim of bullying in primary school, took on a different role in the group in order to save himself from being bullied:

"I became the class idiot: being more rowdy, losing what interest I had in school work: my school work went out the window! The pattern continued through secondary school. I worked on it! I became worse, more of a clown, developing totally disruptive behaviour. I got attention, got a laugh – even became heroic. People talked about me, even people I didn't know. They knew my name: I had a reputation!"

In the end, Stevie was taken into care.

Another aspect of group dynamics is that one child might get blamed for bullying in a group whereas in fact the whole group may be responsible.

Donna: "I must admit that although at first I focussed the blame on one child who physically hit Jo, I now realise it was the whole group who singled him out. I watched them in the playground, watched their body language. When they saw Jo, all their faces would light up, and they'd call, 'Oh, there's Fatface, let's get him'. The whole group was involved in his persecution. Understanding that helped me approach it in a different way with the teachers."

It also made Donna realise that Jo felt insecure in a group situation:

"Because he was quite big and strong, I always thought he could look after himself. From a one-to-one perspective at home, I thought he was adequate in sorting things out. But

at school, a group was a threatening situation for him. We are a small family and he is an only child, not used to group situations. I thought he could cope. I was very slow to pick up that he was being bullied."

Sometimes an 'outsider' to a group may feel left out or picked on, but to the group mentality she or he may be perceived as a threat, or as 'different'. There is a risk of the group turning on her or him just for being in that outsider (or minority) role.

PARENT-CHILD RELATIONSHIP

Whilst often not related to bullying, the relationship between parent and child can affect the social roles a child might play. A child who is constantly ignored, or tyrannised, by a parent, may then bully others in order to get attention or to pass on their pain and humiliation. A child who receives attention only for disruptive behaviour is more likely to behave in a disruptive way. A child who is bullied at home is likely to play a bullying role or may continue to play the victim.

(Note: the idea here is to encourage you as a parent to change your own behaviour if necessary. Just by becoming more conscious of the way you behave can help you make positive changes in the way you relate to your child.)

Eleanor, from a young child, had always felt intimidated by her father:

"My father was a terrible bully. He was a farmer, and bullied his farmworkers, bullied his family."

Even when she was a teenager, staying at home,

Eleanor was forbidden by her father to go out with friends, let alone have boyfriends. When asked to make a comparison between the bullying she experienced at school and her relationship with her father, she said:

"Well, what's more important, eating bread when you're a schoolgirl or having a social life when you're a teenager?"

Chapter Three

IMMEDIATE STRATEGIES

Jim: "Children need help, they have to be brave to talk about such things."

A. WHAT TO DO IF YOU SUSPECT YOUR CHILD IS BEING BULLIED

If you know, or suspect, your child is being bullied, you need to take action. Taking action also requires being able to stay clearheaded. However distressed you and your child may be feeling, you as the adult have to be able to steer a way through the situation. This requires skill and sensitivity, especially if you suspect (but don't know) your child is being bullied.

When we're crossing a road, the first thing we tell our children is to STOP, LOOK, and LISTEN. In the case of bullying, we need to give ourselves the same advice. The best action before, say, confronting the teacher or the parents of the bully is to STOP: think about the situation and LISTEN.

Your first, and very natural response might be to go and 'sort them out' or 'give them a talking to'. You may feel hurt and angry on your child's behalf. Good!

Anger is there for a reason: to fuel you to do what you have to do – that is, to take swift, effective and appropriate action.

i) Communicating with your Child

First, take stock. LOOK at what's going on and consider your options. It may be that you're too upset to think clearly. So, take some time to check out and acknowledge your own feelings, and to comfort the child if she or he seems upset.

Second, LISTEN to your child. Even if your child won't talk, take note of her or his non-verbal communication: body language, posture, facial expressions, and so on. Be guided by the child. If she/he wants to be left alone, respect their right to privacy. If she/he wants to scream and shout, allow that as well. It's healthy to express such feelings. She or he may want to paint or draw or make up a poem – that, too, is an empowering way of release.

Third, the important thing is to let your child know you are there for them, that you believe in them and that you care.

Fourth, if you are worried, say, 'I'm worried', and ask your child directly what's been happening. Avoid asking too many questions, or this may have the opposite effect of making a child clam up!

Acknowledge to the child that you know bullying 'can be scary' and that one of the problems is 'it can be very hard to talk about it'. Let them know that if they do want to talk later, today, another day or any time, you will be available to listen. That way, you 'keep the door open' rather than slam it closed. Convey to the child your belief that talking about it is not 'telling tales' and that everyone – adult or child – has the right to ask for help.

A child (or teenager) who may have been too afraid to say anything for a long time may welcome the opportunity:

Doug (on being discovered playing truant): "Although I'd dreaded being found out, it was such a RELIEF to tell Mum and Dad what was happening. To name names... although very painful and difficult, it was a great relief. My parents were surprised and shocked, though. They told the school and a meeting was arranged between them, the headmaster and myself."

Just being available and listening to our children can help them feel supported. The fact of being heard and believed may not change what has happened, but it lets a child know that you take the situation very seriously. It is important to stress to the child that you know it's not their fault. This may help to alleviate their suffering and restore some of their self-esteem, which may be very eroded, especially if the bullying has been going on for some time. Love and affection are the best remedies.

Fifth, even if you don't know what to do, *say* you don't know!

Stevie (in his teens): "It was one day, when I was sitting on the ramp going up to our flats, that one of my brothers came and sat down next to me, at my level – he just sat there for a while, with his head in his hands, then he turned to me, all emotional, and said, 'Stevie, I don't know what to do.' Although I mocked him at the time, that was a turning point, that's what made a difference. After that, I knew I needed to ask for help. I knew I could ask for help, and that people cared."

Sometimes, a child or teenager may find it easier to talk to another relative or trusted adult. Let them know that that is alright with you; together you might be able to think of someone who would be a good 'mentor'.

ii) Talking to the School

It will be easier to communicate with the school if they have an anti-bullying policy, and if it is working! If so, they should already have procedures in place for reporting and acting on bullying incidents and suspected bullying. In fact, with an effective policy, it should also be easier for children to report bullying at the school. Ask the school if they have an anti-bullying policy, or guidelines on bullying. Different schools proceed in different ways.

If you suspect bullying, talk to the teacher in the first instance. Express your concerns (including any anxieties about risks for the child about 'telling'). Describe what you suspect is going on and what the effects are on your child. State how this makes you feel as well. (If it makes you feel upset or angry, say so.) Ask for the teacher's view of what has been happening. Listen to what she or he says, even if you don't agree. It's important to establish a dialogue.

Let the teacher know you want any bullying

stopped immediately. She or he should agree to look into the matter and to keep a watchful eye on your child. This could include alerting other staff (teachers, playground supervisors etc). Ask for assurances about your child's safety and arrange a follow-up meeting to check progress.

Even if you're not entirely satisfied with the teacher's response, accept any offers of help made. This may just be the starting point in the struggle against bullying, and it's important to establish co-operation.

B. WHAT TO DO IF YOU KNOW YOUR CHILD IS BEING BULLIED

i) Talking to Your Child

If you know for certain that your child is being bullied, reassure your child that you take it very seriously and that the bullying has to stop. Let them know you care about them and that you know it's not their fault. Follow the STOP, LOOK, LISTEN steps at the beginning of this chapter. It may well be that both you and your child are suffering from shock. Take time to be together and recover your strength. Help your child feel valued and special – their self-esteem has probably been severely dented. Decide together what action needs to be taken.

ii) Talking to the School

If there has been a serious incident of physical bullying where your child has suffered severe injury, loss or damage to property, you are advised to report it immediately to the school – by telephone if necessary in the first instance, followed by a visit in person. Or, if it has taken place outside the school, to the police. Take photographs of injuries and write down dates of any hospital visits or visits to the doctor. Keep your child off school, if necessary. This is legitimate so long as you have a doctor's note.

If the school has an effective anti-bullying policy, you can expect full co-operation from teachers and pastoral staff and procedures in place to be followed as soon as bullying is reported. If not, a lot will depend on individual teachers and your own attitude. It's important to be assertive, not aggressive. Not too meek, either:

Donna: "On several occasions I spoke to the Head and teachers, but it didn't seem to have much effect. I think I tried to be casual, matter-of-fact. But I was too polite! The last time, I lost my temper, really let my feelings show – not abusive but angry, and argumentative, laying it on the line, showing I meant it... My son was coming home with his shirt covered in blood and nasty grazes on his elbow from being pushed on the ground – I was absolutely fed up, absolutely had enough. THEY GOT THE MESSAGE!"

Say you want the bullying stopped and the incident investigated. The chances are that the bullying may be affecting many children. Ask what support and supervision your child will be offered. (Where there is adequate supervision, there is generally less bullying.) Ask how your child's safety can be guaranteed and what action, if any, will be taken against the bullies. Arrange another meeting to monitor progress.

Keep a note of the dates you visit the school and the

names of staff spoken to. Go to see the Headteacher if necessary. You may also want to contact your local borough's Education Welfare Officer. If you are still not satisfied, write a letter to the School Governors. Insist you will not be satisfied until the bullying has stopped.

How the school reacts could also depend on your child's relationship with the teacher.

Jennifer: "Some of the staff were very offputting. I had to go and see the Headteacher. She seemed understanding and said 'I have a lot of time for Lorraine.' That made all the difference. Lorraine was on the verge of being pushed out – we thought the answer would be for her to leave school at 16. But after that she stayed on and did alright in the sixth form."

Molly (Sharon's mother) was not so fortunate: "The teacher seemed not very bothered about her – I think it's because of something that happened in the past when she got a bit of a reputation of being a bit 'uppity'. But it really upset me to think that no one in authority seemed to be keeping 'an eye out for her' – anything could have happened. I got very, very angry with the teacher."

Even if your child and teacher don't like each other, you and your child still have the right to have the bullying stopped. Kate, a teacher, advises parents to remain as calm as possible when talking to the teachers.

"Try not to lay blame on anybody," she says. "State what has been happening to your child and how it makes you feel, as well as the effect it has been having on your child."

She does, however, recognise that this is exceedingly difficult for parents sometimes:

"Even if a parent goes 'over the top', a teacher needs to

recognise they've got a real difficulty."

Her advice to teachers is:

"Don't get defensive. Acknowledge parents' feelings. Acknowledge your <u>own</u> feelings. This helps to diffuse the situation. Then at least you can talk about it."

iii) How the School Will Proceed

Depending on their anti-bullying policy (or not) different schools will handle the situation in different ways. Generally, a meeting is arranged between teaching staff and bullies and the victim separately. Witnesses may be interviewed as well. Action may have to be taken to break up bully gangs. In some schools the bullies will be punished, in others sanctions imposed against them. They may be made to apologise or compensate the victim in some way.

Some schools adopt a 'no-blame' approach that involves consulting bullies as well as victims and other children in finding solutions to the problem, the principle being that giving responsibility to the bullies is more likely to help them change their behaviour than punishing them. It also recognises that sometimes many children have been involved in the problem, as witnesses or as victims or as bullies or onlookers.

Counselling or guidance may be on offer for the victim from the pastoral care worker or Educational Psychologist or School Counsellor. Sometimes, depending on the degree of bullying and the effectiveness of the school, some of these measures may already have been taken by the school without the parents knowing. Sometimes threatening to summon parents to the school is enough of a deterrent!

There are positive and inspiring initiatives now in many schools, helping the whole school community overcome bullying. You may be pleasantly surprised.

iv) Special Needs
If the bullying is about a particular issue, for example the special needs of a child, or a specific disability, or a specific problem (such as a parent in prison) it may be helpful to mount an education programme with the children about the issue, whilst not focussing attention on a particular child.

C. STRATEGIES FOR YOUR CHILD

1. Your child may not want you to tell anyone else they have been involved in bullying. Explain to your child that it's important to tell people in order to stop the bullying. Reassure your child that you will help them sort out their problem. Older children and teenagers, especially, may be acutely sensitive to any intervention and prefer to deal with it themselves. You might be able to help her/him think up some ways of telling the teacher her/himself. Then practise saying it with them, to help them feel more confident.

To counteract the stigma of 'telling', it might be helpful to say to your child that there is no shame in having a problem. Life is full of problems and how we handle them is what helps us and others grow. What is shameful is having to suffer in silence.

2. Your child's safety is paramount. Do not advise them to 'hit back' or to try to take on the bullies themselves. Together, think of ways they could avoid the bullies or the bullying situation, for example by staying with other friends at break (safety in numbers) or even having one close friend so they're not on their own at playtime.

Keep your child informed of any meetings you have with the school. Let them know what provisions may be being made there for their safety.

Shana: "Now the gang is being monitored at playtime, and they <u>know</u> they're being monitored. Also, Kanushi spends less time on her own now, plays with a friend. Since she's been playing with someone else, there have been no bruises."

and:

Donna: "Jo never liked football anyway. Now he plays with a different crowd, with different interests. He's much happier now, full of beans."

3. Help your child learn to ignore comments or teasing, however hurtful it may be. Often the bullies are *trying* to get a reaction, and your child's response may affect whether they decide to bully or not. Getting upset, or responding with more name-calling, only encourages them.

Help your child practise a response to name-calling, if you and your child think this would be helpful. Together you can practise telling the bullies to 'back off', or words to that effect, but you must say it angrily to have effect and *walk away immediately*. Sometimes it is useful to have a reply prepared. Giving a short, fairly neutral retort, such as 'maybe, maybe not' or 'I don't think so' can also help to deflect insults. Practise saying it in the mirror!

4. Advise your child not to take valuable possessions to school or to linger alone in changing rooms or corridors, and, if confronted, to walk away immediately and keep walking, and seek help if necessary.

5. Some parents find that 'role playing' the situation with their child helps. This is where the child describes the situation and they enact it together, with the adult playing the part of the bully, or their child: the roles are interchangeable. This way the situation can be run and re-run, trying different attitudes and responses. It helps the child feel more powerful and equipped to deal with the situation again should it arise. (It could also be used to practise approaching the teacher.)

Bob: "Deborah enjoys it, and asks for it again now, as needed!"

6. It may be that your child is bullied wherever she or he goes. This suggests they may be a 'perpetual victim' and doing something which attracts bullying behaviour towards them. Are they very timid? Do they have a very 'needy' body posture? There may be something in their behaviour – for example an obnoxious habit or annoying mannerism or just undeveloped social skills – that you may be able to help them change. For example, a child who has an unfortunate habit of barging into groups may be able to practise *asking* if she can join in. Again, role play may help. But whatever the reason, the bullying has to be stopped. And remember, we are all unique, with different traits and characters and cultures and backgrounds, with different abilities and gifts – whilst we can help a child modify their behaviour, it is unfair to expect our children to become anything other than who they are! In the next chapter, we look at ways of helping children build self-confidence.

There is never any justification for bullying. Helping our children overcome bullying will increase their chances to fulfil their true potential.

D. What To Do If You Suspect (Or Know) Your Child Is Being A Bully

If you suspect your child of bullying, or if others have accused her or him:

1. Take the same steps mentioned at the beginning of this chapter of STOP, LOOK and LISTEN.

Bullying behaviour is often a symptom of a child feeling deeply troubled – it may be a cry for help. Children who are bullying often deny there's anything wrong, however.

Conversely, sometimes children don't *know* how much hurt they're causing. Explain their bullying behaviour to them – for instance, get them to imagine how they would feel if they were in the victim's shoes. Teach them empathy.

Sometimes, with young children especially, their bullying behaviour may be just waiting for an adult to come along and tell them off... Children *need* clear boundaries for their behaviour, and sometimes that is all it takes for them to change the behaviour.

2. Avoid rushing into punitive action – for example, giving the child a beating. This will only make the problem worse. Aggression breeds more aggression, and the child may take it out on someone else.

3. It is vital to confront your child and look the issue in the eye. However uncomfortable or painful this may be for you, it is a lot worse for the victim. The bullying must stop. Make it very clear that it is totally unacceptable behaviour.

If your child admits to being guilty, let them know they still have rights (for a 'fair hearing'etc). Even quite young children can feel a strong sense of 'it's not fair' and, although admitting responsibility for their own actions, they might feel they're also carrying the can for others.

Let them know that it is their *behaviour* that is unacceptable, that behaviour can be changed and that you still love them as a person.

4. Ask yourself why your child is bullying. Recognise that they may be suffering from very low self-esteem. Their behaviour may have arisen from emotional distress, of feelings of inadequacy or feeling unloved or ignored. It may be a way of coping with family difficulties or the trauma of being bullied themselves. Or they may be struggling with school work, possibly needing help with a learning difficulty. Are they over or under-achieving at school?

5. LISTEN to your child's side of the story. Who else was involved? Why did it happen? Take time and really listen. Your child needs to feel supported, and to know that you care.

6. Offer support to help your child change their behaviour. *Ask* what would help. Children and teenagers are very good at thinking up their own solutions, given half a chance, and of stating what they need, given encouragement and permission to do so.

Even if they say something outlandish at first, like, 'The only thing that would help me would be a one-way ticket to the moon', there might be an element of truth in it: for example, the implied message being, 'What I really need is to get away from this situation and this group of people'.

7. Find out all sides of the story. Talk to other parents/playground supervisor etc, to find out their side of the story as well. Build up a picture of what has been going on.

8. Discuss with your child the effects on the victim and possible ways of making it up to her or him.

9. Talk to the school. With your child (or teenager), talk to the teacher. 'Come clean' and say s/he is committed to changing their behaviour, and will need support. State what kind of support, and stay in contact with the teacher, to monitor progress. If there have been family problems, be as honest about these as possible.

Louise: "I was labelled the bully of my class. I was bigger than everybody and they used to wind me up so much, I <u>used</u>

my size and really hurt them, sometimes. Not all the time, though I was always the one called out by the teachers if there was any trouble. I used to get so angry and upset! Then one day, a teacher said to me, 'Louise, why don't you go into that empty classroom for a while and cool down?' She offered me a refuge! From that day on, my life began to change. I can never thank her enough..."

10. Together you and your child could consider some alternatives to their present situation: for example, join an activity group, take up new interests and make new friends. Go on a holiday? You may have to invest some time and energy in them for a while, on a daily basis: support with school work, encouraging creativity, going on outings, etc.

11. Give your child opportunities to excel, in whatever they're good at, in order to help them feel good about themselves.

12. Another strategy to help children who bully is to help them learn assertive, rather than aggressive behaviour. It is never too soon (or too late) to learn about boundaries and that the way to get something is not to hurt someone. Ideally, children are taught this *before* they go to school!

As a parent, you, too, may need to practise assertive behaviour on your child. Practise saying 'no' and setting boundaries.

13. If you are worried that your child's bullying behaviour is severe, you may need to seek professional help. Talk to the Educational Psychologist in the first instance, or your local borough's Education Welfare Officer. See also 'Useful Addresses' at the back of this book.

SUPPORT FOR YOURSELF

At the beginning of the chapter, we looked at ways of supporting your child. In the same way, it would help you as the parent or carer to get support for *yourself* at this time. Talk to your partner, if you have one, or a counsellor or friend – someone you trust, and who will be able to listen in confidence and enable you to share your feelings. It can be a very confusing time for you and your child, and sometimes just being listened to in an empathic way can feel more supportive than any wealth of advice. It may also help you to separate your own 'issues' from your child's. Remember, the more support you get for yourself, the more support you will be able to give your child.

Chapter Four

LONG-TERM STRATEGIES

It is necessary to help build self-esteem and confidence in your child in order to overcome bullying long-term. This applies whether your child has been a bully or a victim. If she or he has been a victim, it will help restore confidence and empower her or him to resist, or prevent bullying in the future. It will help them 'stick up for themselves', not in the sense of fighting but in standing up non-physically to the threat of bullying and in developing a sense of *inner* strength, *inner* power. Because bullying is the exercise of power over others, having a sense of one's own inner power helps to deflect bullying.

If your child has been a bully, helping him or her build their self-esteem and confidence should reduce the *need* for bullying behaviour. The more a child, or teenager, feels a sense of inner power, the less reason he or she will have to bully others in order to feel powerful.

EMPOWERING THE CHILD

The most effective way to help a child develop inner strength is to enable her or him to feel confident in their abilities and to feel loved and valued. This can be done by giving encouragement, support and positive attention.

• Help her or him feel good about themselves. That way they learn that, if another child doesn't like them, that's the *other* child's problem. Help children realise that most people feel bad about themselves some days and good on others: feeling good about yourself doesn't mean feeling good all the time.

• Help your child feel special, just for being who they are!

• Give your child responsibility – ask her/him to help you in tasks around the house or garden that she or he is able to achieve. That will help to make her/him feel valued and successful.

• Give encouragement and approval. If you feel the need to criticise or tell your child off about something, do so in a *constructive* way: for example, by saying what it is about their *behaviour* that you don't like, rather than making them feel bad as a person. As well as preserving their self-esteem, this will help them learn how to communicate to *others* about unacceptable behaviour.

• Set clear boundaries. Children, and teenagers, need boundaries to feel secure, as well as to push against. Children need to learn, from a very early age, that certain behaviour is unacceptable. Boundaries change, of course, at different ages and stages. As children grow older, they become more able to set their own boundaries, given help and responsibility to do so. In teenage years, especially, this sometimes requires hard negotiation!

• If your child has been a bully, it may take time for her or him to change their bullying behaviour, especially if it had become a habit. There may be setbacks, especially if others (in the gang, for example) who associate them in the bullying role don't want them to change. Help your child resist taunts or mocking and give encouragement and approval for their efforts to change.

• Help your child make new friends.

• Encourage special interests. If your child has a particular hobby or interest, help her/him find ways of developing their interest and skills. It's also a way of meeting new friends.

• Give your child time to recover. If she/he has been a victim of bullying, it may take time to regain confidence. Whilst developing new interests and meeting new friends will help recovery, allow her or him to do so at their own pace.

In other words, don't push them!

• Value your child's feelings. If she or he feels upset or angry, allow them to express their feelings. Say, 'You seem upset about that' rather than deny the upset by saying, 'Don't be silly, there's nothing to be upset about'...

• Value your own feelings. If you're angry, say, 'I'm angry!' without making it all the child's fault.

• Give attention to positive behaviour in children. It's a well known fact from child psychologists that children will develop behaviour to get 'negative attention' rather than no attention at all.

• Trust in your child's ability. Let your child *feel* that you have confidence in their abilities. Don't become *over*-protective. This can take *away* a child's power. It's hard, sometimes, finding the balance between *necessary* protection and enabling a child to take responsibility her/himself.

Keep working at it! This is one of the challenges of being a parent.

• Find out about self-assertiveness courses for children (and adults) in your area. Your local library should have details.

• Find out about self-defence classes. These may help your child feel stronger, both physically and mentally. The idea is not so much to turn her/him into a super-hero as to increase their confidence and help them be *aware* of their strength.

• Recognise that feelings change. Each of us can feel vulnerable one day, and strong the next. Help your child realise that no one feels 'tough' all the time. Bullies can feel frightened as well, even if they don't show it.

• Help your child make friends. If she/he doesn't seem to have friends, it might help to invite a child or two home. (Not a group, in case they gang up on her or him.) If a teenager, s/he might need encouragement to join a club or special interest group to meet new friends.

• Help your child make changes: for example, to overcome anti-social behaviour. She or he might have a tendency to 'show off' or be a nuisance to others. Such behaviour might have originated in early childhood, as a way of attention-seeking. However, she or he may need to be given help in learning new behaviour.

Norah, a school pastoral care worker: "One girl who got bullied always used to barge into groups of children in the playground. We helped her find ways of going up to a group and asking to join in."

Role play and other exercises can help.

Sometimes, children who are 'on the fringes' need help with learning how to play with other children.

However, some children who are outside the group are *not* bullied. For some children, it's not a problem being outside the group, unless adults make it a problem!

• Help your child feel secure, especially if going through changes at home or through a change of school. Take time, if possible, to support them through the transition, and talk about your feelings, and theirs about the changes that are happening.

Starting school for the first time can be a traumatic time for parents as well as children. It is important for parents to help children prepare for such a major transition. It is hard, sometimes, for parents to adjust to the separation. You may need to seek help for yourself, then it will be easier for you to help your child feel secure in the transition.

TAKE AN INTEREST IN THEIR SCHOOL

Whether your child is in primary or secondary school, take an interest in what she or he is being taught. As well as helping your child feel supported and encouraged, you might learn a thing or two yourself! It means you can also check on academic progress and pick up on any learning difficulties that may arise – for example, difficulties or blocks with reading or writing – where she or he may need extra support. Extra support is available in many schools. Such difficulties can cause enormous frustration in children, and sometimes lead to bullying: either bullying of a child with learning difficulties, or bullying *by* a child with learning difficulties, as a way of compensating for feeling inadequate and/or as a means of expressing the frustration.

Learning difficulties can cause frustration, as well, in adults. Some schools operate 'family learning' schemes to help parents and children learn together (literacy and numeracy, for example). There are also excellent courses in adult education colleges for almost every subject under the sun, from computer literacy to music and art. Free yourself of your own blocks!

You might find your child is over-achieving through too much pressure (do you have too high expectations of your child?), or under-achieving because her/his level of ability is not being matched. If this is the case, you might have to consider other outlets for your child to express and develop her/his talents.

LEARNING ENVIRONMENT

Create a learning environment at home. This doesn't mean turning your living room into a library (just turning your kitchen into a study!). It means taking time, sometimes, to talk and listen to your child and take an interest and talk about life, the universe (and everything!). Given the pressures of being a parent, it may not be possible to give a lot of time, but even making a commitment to *some* time, perhaps a regular 'slot' each day, (perhaps sitting down to read or study in the same room while they're doing their homework) will make a difference. Children, and teenagers, learn by example. If they see you enjoying (and grappling with!) learning, they are more likely to follow. (Note: if your children are at boarding school, make sure you create a learning environment during the holidays.)

EMPOWERING THE PARENT

Bullying behaviour, and the vulnerability that puts children at risk of being bullied, is sometimes a symptom of extreme stress in children. Many children feel under stress because their *parents* are stressed, and unable to give them (the children) much attention. Stress seems to be a symptom of our society, and being a parent can be a complex and demanding role, often juggling different needs and struggling with lack of time or lack of money. It's hard to help our children feel secure when we're feeling insecure ourselves. How we manage stress and how we manage our own and our children's needs is paramount in helping ourselves, and our children feel confident and secure. It also helps us to take care of our own, and our children's physical and mental health.

There are many ways to alleviate stress. Most of us have developed our own favourite strategies. It might be soaking in a hot bath by candlelight, or going for a run in the park. Or just having a good laugh! Massage, yoga and meditation all help to dissolve tension and re-connect us with our inner strength. (See your local library or adult education college for details of courses.) What matters is making a *commitment* to ourselves to make time regularly for this. Make it a priority, in the same way that, in order to keep a car running, you have to keep the battery charged!

It may be that your child is in a more vulnerable state than usual, or more prone to bullying behaviour, because of a crisis at home or family problems. There may have been a bereavement in the family, or a divorce, or a separation, or there may be changes in your family situation – a move, for example, or the arrival of a new baby, or other major adjustments such as becoming part of a step-family. If so, you may need to seek help for *yourself*, in order to help you and your family manage the changes. There are many wonderful organisations that offer support and self-help and bring together others who may be going through a similar situation. (See list of Useful Addresses at the end of the book.)

Problems are part of life, and how you approach, and resolve problems sets an example for your child. Seeing you take action rather than being a 'victim' to circumstances will benefit your child. Even if you can't change circumstances, you can change your responses to them and find solutions to problems. And if you turn to appropriate channels of help, your child will learn that:

a) it's all right to seek help, and
b) help is available.

PARENT POWER IN THE COMMUNITY

Bullying is a community issue. As well as affecting the school community, it reflects the community at large. Many parents feel vulnerable and isolated in the community, and worried about the risks to their children. They fear that no one in the community is 'keeping an eye out' for them. In the days of television, and of mobility, where parents often live far away from other members of their family, it is true that communities are often fragmented and support is often lacking.

That is why, for parents and children to feel supported, it is vital to form networks of support in the community. This in itself helps to build a stronger community. So, talk to other parents about bullying. Talk to other parents about anything! Go to meetings of the PTA (Parent Teacher Association) and share your concerns. This will help you build relationships with other parents and teachers and make it easier to discuss any other issues that may arise in the future.

If your child's school doesn't have an anti-bullying policy, you and other parents could possibly put pressure on the school to create one. Or, you could help to create one. For an anti-bullying policy to be effective, it really needs input from all sectors of the school community: parents, teachers, non-teaching staff and, last but not least, the pupils! The most successful anti-bullying campaigns have all included the children in finding solutions. (See Useful Addresses at the back of the book for organisations that provide information on creating anti-bullying policies.)

Obviously, any anti-bullying policy should also reflect school policy on what is acceptable and unacceptable behaviour in school.

It may be that you have very negative associations with school from your own school days. You are not alone! But it is important for you to overcome these if you want to play a more active role in your child's education and well-being at school. Teachers often welcome parental involvement. Sometimes parents are unaware of that, or are reluctant to go to the school, or don't know how to become involved. Nowadays, with increasing talk about 'partnership' between parents and schools, it is worth asking the school how you can be involved. That way you may increase the sense of partnership between you and your child and help your child feel more of a sense of belonging to the school community.

IF THE BULLYING CONTINUES

i) Taking It Further
If bullying continues and you are not satisfied with the school's response, you may wish to consider taking the matter further. You could contact the Board of Governors (or the School Board if a Scottish school). If you are still not satisfied, you can complain in writing to the Local Director of Education (your town or county hall can give you the name). If the matter is not dealt with speedily, contact your town or county councillor, or your MP.

If you make no progress, and the bullying continues, you might have to consider sending your child to another school.

You also have the right to educate your child at home yourself. (See 'Education Otherwise' under Useful Addresses at the end of this book.) Think very carefully before choosing this option! It works well for some families, who raise well-balanced and well-educated children. However, it obviously puts more responsibility and pressure on a parent or parents who may already be under considerable constraints of time and energy. It only works well if a parent and others have enough time and attention to give to the child. Children require a lot of attention and stimulation for learning. They also need adequate social contact, which a school provides, to develop their interpersonal and social skills.

ii) Changing School

If this doesn't work, or if your child still seems unhappy at school, it may be that a change of school would be the best option for your child. Even if that seems an unlikely option, it is always good to know that other options are available. Discuss other possibilities with your child. Sometimes, just being given choices can make a difference to a child (and an adult!). Often, given a choice, a child will want to stay where they are rather than face a new, unknown situation. Even deciding that is a choice, which may help them make a fresh commitment to their present schooling.

Matthew: "Sally does all her homework now and seems really committed to her education since we had the talk about her changing school. She still gets wound up by the boys in her class sometimes, but nothing like as bad as before. I don't know if they're behaving any better or if she just doesn't let them get to her any more. She seems to have put the whole thing in perspective – she wants to get her GCSEs and even enjoys school quite a lot."

Eleanor, however, would have been only too glad to leave her school, given half a chance:

"I just didn't want to be there. My ideal solution would have been for my parents to take me out of school altogether. I would have been quite happy to stay at home and study on my own."

As it happened, when Eleanor was ill and had to spend several weeks at home, her father gave her two hours' tuition every day before starting work on the farm. They got up at four each morning. The rest of the day she worked alone. When she returned to school, the teachers were astounded at her progress.

Eleanor: "The truth is, I was deeply unhappy at school. I would have liked to have been asked, 'What would you like to do? What school, if any, would you like to go to?' I think children should be given choices – let them know there are options. Give some responsibility to the child, even though the parent has responsibility for the decision."

BULLYING IN THE FAMILY

i) Brothers and Sisters

You may have to consider strategies for dealing with bullying in the family. Do older brothers or sisters gang up on a younger member of the family? If so, how do you handle this? Do you think it's 'just part of family life' or do you intervene? Can you distinguish between normal 'sibling rivalry' and bullying behaviour? You may have to take firm action in order to stop bullying behaviour and make it clear to your children that such behaviour is unacceptable.

Even 'normal' sibling rivalry can be difficult enough to deal with. Sometimes the best strategy then is to leave children to sort out their conflicts on their own, intervening only to prevent them from harming each other if an argument escalates into a fight. Try to avoid taking sides.

Support them in finding their own solutions by

asking: 'How are you going to resolve this?' This empowers them to take responsibility.

PARENTING STYLES

It is worth considering your own relationship with your child, or children, in seeking long-term approaches to bullying. As a parent, do you behave aggressively to your child or children? Do you constantly tease, or ignore him or her? Or do you rush to 'rescue' her or him at every opportunity, making her/him feel a constant victim?

We saw in an earlier chapter how family dynamics can be an influencing factor in how a child behaves, or is treated at school. Children often learn bullying or victim behaviour at home. Developing a positive relationship with your child is paramount in helping your child overcome bullying.

Take time to reflect on your own style of parenting. It might be 'authoritarian' – that is, being completely controlling of your child and allowing her or him very little responsibility for their own choices and actions. An over-controlling style of parenting can lead to timid *or* rebellious behaviour in a child. A child treated aggressively at home is more likely to behave aggressively towards others at school.

On the other hand, you may have a 'permissive' style of parenting, where 'anything goes' – letting your child or children do more or less what they want. This can lead to disruptive behaviour in children because they lack boundaries, and may even be being disruptive in order to *feel* some boundaries to push against. Boundaries help children and teenagers feel secure. Do your children bully you? If so, this could be a symptom of over-permissive parenting. The other side of the permissiveness coin is that, far from feeling 'free spirits', children may feel ignored and neglected and rejected, feelings that they may carry with them into school and putting them more at risk of being bullied.

The reality is, that for most of us, our parenting style lies somewhere between these extremes. And styles can fluctuate. Most of us are quite tolerant as parents, and every now and then lose our tolerance – and our temper – completely! But it helps us and our children if we become more conscious of our general style of parenting so that we can make adjustments if we want to. Also, we need to be able to adapt our style to suit the different styles and temperaments of our children!

It is vital to stress the importance, here, of appreciating ourselves as parents and recognising how much we have done for our children, rather than blaming ourselves for our mistakes. It's almost inevitable, given the power imbalance between parents and children, that we will all have bullied our children at some time, emotionally if not physically. 'If you don't clear up that mess I'll...' is a form of intimidation. 'If you do anything to upset me I won't love you any more' is a strong threat, often delivered not in so many words but as an implied message that parents give their children.

It is never too late to change patterns if we want to, and, as mentioned already, there are many courses available specifically for parents to help them develop new strategies and skills. (See Useful Addresses at the end of the book.) This is a more positive approach to improving relationships with our children than 'beating ourselves up' (bullying ourselves)!

Chapter Five

SKILLS

Jim: "If only they had listened to me, not just when the bad things happened but listened to how I was at other times, taken some interest, <u>understood</u> what was going on in my life..."

The purpose of this chapter is to help you and your child develop skills in communication and assertiveness that may make it easier to stand up against bullying and to prevent bullying behaviour.

It might also make it easier for you to communicate with your child about bullying. How we communicate, as parents, affects the way our children communicate with us, and can make all the difference to the way we handle a situation.

Communication is also the most powerful weapon against bullying and, of course, against denial.

TALKING AND LISTENING

A child who is bullied is likely to be withdrawn and fearful and not want to talk about it, thus increasing the sense of isolation for both child and parent.

One of the best ways to encourage a child to talk is to be available to *listen*. This means not just sitting down to hear what she or he has to say (if anything!) about bullying, but developing the habit of listening at other times, and about anything the child wants to talk about. This doesn't mean giving your child undivided attention the whole time (for most parents this would be impossible!) but letting your child feel that they do have your undivided attention, sometimes. (It also helps if you sit with them at their own level, rather than towering above them.)

A child who feels listened to is more likely to feel supported and valued, and have confidence in you as a listener. This will make it easier for her or him to 'open up' about painful or difficult issues if necessary.

Some suggestions about listening:

• Get into the habit of listening.

• Give feedback to let the child know you have heard what she/he has said. For example, 'You're saying you don't like potatoes/swimming/Peter?'

• Allow the child to talk freely without interrupting. Listening skills require the ability to give full attention, in a non-judgemental way, rather than engaging in argument or conversation.

• Ask open-ended questions rather than 'closed' questions. A closed question is one that demands 'yes' or 'no' as the answer. For example, 'Did you steal that pencil?' or, 'Did Hannah push you?' This limits the response a child can give, and may lead to more denial. It is more useful to phrase questions such as, 'WHAT happened about the pencil?' or 'HOW did you get hurt?' thus allowing the child more opportunity to talk about their experience and be truthful.

• Agree to keep confidentiality.

• Disclose your own feelings. For example, say, 'I'm feeling anxious/worried/concerned...'. This leaves responsibility with you and helps take the pressure off the child. (If you feel very anxious but don't say so, the child will probably sense the anxiety anyway, and feel it is their fault.)

• Set time limits if necessary. For example, 'This is important, and I'm very busy at the moment. Let's talk about it again later.' (Set a time, and try to keep to it.)
    If your child discloses that there has been bullying or abuse, let her/him know you take it very seriously. Give assurances that you will help her/him put an end to it. Say that you might have to break confidentiality for their own protection.

TALKING ABOUT FEELINGS

Part of being able to listen to, and accept your child's experience, is being able to accept your child's feelings. If your child says she/he is frightened, and you say, 'Don't be silly' or, 'There's nothing to be frightened of', you are invalidating your child's feelings. It is more helpful to the child if you are able to let them know you have heard them say they are frightened. Then you can give them any reassurance they need.

Another way of helping your child talk about their feelings is to set an example by talking about your own feelings. You can practise doing this in any situation: for example, walking in the park: 'When I see dog mess it makes me feel angry,' or watching television: 'I feel sad watching this programme... I feel sad when I see people hurt each other.' You could also ask them, 'How does it make you feel?'

EXPRESSING FEELINGS

As well as talking about feelings, it is important for a child to be allowed to express emotions such as sadness, frustration or anger. Feelings are an important part of life, for both children and adults, and give meaning to our experience. If feelings are ignored, or 'pushed down', this can lead to denial of the experience. Feelings being denied over a long period of time can lead to depression and ill health (mental as well as physical).

Help your child learn that she/he is entitled to their feelings and that it is healthy to express them, so long as doing so does not physically harm themselves or others. Validate your child's feelings by letting her/him know that if they are hurt, it's only natural to feel upset.

Sometimes, bullying behaviour can be a symptom of unexpressed feelings being kept down, suppressed. A child or teenager who feels a great deal of emotional pain, for example, may hurt others in an attempt to avoid the pain. For that child, bullying others may almost be a way of attacking the feelings themselves.

IF A CHILD IS UPSET

If a child is upset, the best support you can give is to be acknowledging and accepting of their feelings. Even saying 'you're sad' or 'you're upset' (rather than 'cheer up' or 'stop crying' or 'boys don't cry') may help. Tears may have to flow before they can subside, and accepting that your child is upset helps the emotion take its course. Acceptance helps a child feel valued and supported and more able to cope, or talk about their experience. Acceptance may also help the upset pass more quickly. We can probably all think of instances where we felt upset about something, and where denial by others led to our feeling even more upset!

There may be times, of course, when a child is upset and you need to take immediate action – for example, if a child is physically hurt, or in crisis.

If you and your children are undergoing a difficult family situation, such as divorce or separation, or adjusting to a move, acknowledge their feelings and your own.

Say that, 'It's painful', or, 'It's difficult', or, 'Things feel uncertain at the moment...' Depending on the severity of the situation, it may help you to have some professional counselling. Or if there has been a bereavement in the family it may help to have some bereavement counselling.

(See Useful Addresses at the end of the book.)

EXPRESSING ANGER

Anger can be a very frightening emotion because it is so powerful. We may be afraid of losing control when we're angry, or of being hurt by others when they are angry.

Many of us were brought up by our own parents to believe that it was 'wrong' to get angry as children. We may even have been punished for being angry. However, anger, like all other feelings, serves a purpose. It helps to connect us to our inner truth and gives us strength to act in situations that we find unacceptable.

We need to be able to allow our children to express their anger, if they need to, and to help them learn to express it in ways that do not harm themselves or others.

AT SCHOOL

A child may need help with managing their anger, or their temper at school, or in other places where it is inappropriate to express it. Help her/him to recognise when they *start* to feel angry, or when they're *about* to lose their temper, so that they can remove themselves from the situation if necessary, and take a few deep breaths to help to 'cool off'. Sometimes going for a run or some other physical activity helps to discharge tension.

AT HOME

Make sure that you and your child take time regularly to relax. Anger is often caused by a build-up of tension.

In the same way as a child who is upset may be helped by having her/his feelings accepted, a child who is angry may feel supported by having her/his angry feelings acknowledged. Saying 'you're angry' may fuel the flames for a moment, but then the anger is more likely to burn out and illuminate communication than if you make the child feel bad for feeling angry. This could make her/him feel more angry!

If a child, or teenager, or adult is very angry, and liable to get violent, then obviously you must put your safety first and get out of the way. There are times when it is *not* appropriate to stay and acknowledge feelings!

It may be that *you* need help in dealing with your anger in appropriate ways, especially if you have a tendency to 'take it out' on the children. One strategy that helps is to be aware of the difference between 'clean' anger, where you clearly state that you're angry and what you are angry about, without blaming anyone, and 'dumping', where you 'dump' your anger on others and make them feel responsible.

A 'clean' expression of anger would be to say (or shout): 'I'm angry about this mess', whereas an example of 'dumping' would be to say (or scream): 'You horrible children, you've done it again' (accompanied, possibly, by a clip round the ears). Most of us are guilty of 'dumping' at some time or another. However, you may need to seek help if that, or violence is a recurring pattern. There are support groups and organisations that help adults overcome violence in the home. There is also a wealth of assertiveness classes, that help people learn to express anger in an assertive, rather than aggressive way.

ASSERTIVENESS

Training in assertiveness skills can boost self-esteem and confidence in both adults and children. It can help both become more effective and less aggressive, or less passive, in their interactions with others.

Children who know how to act assertively may be more able to stand up against bullying. Like the other skills mentioned in this chapter, the best way for us to teach our children the skills is to learn them ourselves and lead by example.

Generally, there are three main styles of responding to a situation: passive, aggressive and assertive. (There is a fourth style – manipulative – which usually belongs in the aggressive category because it is understood to be 'passive aggression' – that is, indirect rather than direct aggression.) Most of us use a combination of these different styles at different times and in different situations. However, we probably have a tendency towards one style more than another.

Bullying is obviously aggressive behaviour (whether direct or indirect), whereas a victim of bullying is likely to be responding in a passive manner. That is not to say that bully or victim are aggressive or passive all the time. But the more *aware* we become of how we are behaving at any time, the more able we are to switch from aggressive or passive to *assertive* behaviour.

Assertive behaviour means being able to state your needs while still respecting that the other person has needs as well. It means being able to say clearly what you want and what you *don't* want. It means knowing you have personal rights: to safety, to being heard, and to stating your needs, even if they can't necessarily be met at the time. It means recognising other people's rights: to safety, to being heard and to stating *their* needs even though they can't necessarily be met at the time.

In the power imbalance between bully and victim, the bully is aggressor and the victim passive, or submissive. In assertiveness, the balance of power is equal. I can say what 'I' need, and I can listen to what 'you' need. It doesn't mean that you or I get what we need at the expense of each other. It means that it is possible to communicate and negotiate. It may mean a compromise has to be reached, but at least there is room to manoeuvre.

Assertiveness is an *attitude* as much as any words that are spoken:

Shashi: "When I told myself I had the right to walk down the corridor, as much right as anybody — I felt stronger. I looked the bullies in the eye and kept walking. They moved out of my way and I walked past them!"

ASSERTIVE STATEMENTS

Making a statement or a request assertively entails more than just the words we say. To be effective, we have to feel assertive and match our body language and facial expression to the words that are being spoken. (This is called being 'congruent'.) For example, if you say, 'I don't want you to do that,' while smiling and walking away, the other person is not likely to take much notice.

As well as being congruent, it is important to hold our ground. If, when we state our needs the other person argues or diverts the conversation to something else, we need to be able to calmly repeat our assertive statement or request. And keep on repeating it, if necessary! When you are satisfied they have *heard* you (though not necessarily agreed to your request), you can then agree to listen to what *they* want, as appropriate.

You and your child might find role play useful in order to practise assertive responses to different situations. (This includes everyday, not just bullying situations.) Play with ideas, and give each other marks out of ten for effectiveness (and congruence), if that helps. Playing different characters can be helpful, as well as fun.

MAKING REQUESTS

• Be clear about what you need or want. For example, 'I want this behaviour to stop.' Or, 'I need some help with carrying the shopping.'

• Say how the behaviour makes you feel. For example, 'When you shout at me I feel hurt.'

• 'Own' feelings – that is, instead of saying, 'You make me angry' say, 'I'm angry'. Or, 'I'm confused', or 'I'm upset about this'. Or: 'I'm happy'!

• State how you feel *and* what you want (or don't want) to happen. For example, 'I'm annoyed that you left me to clear up, and in future I want you to clear up your own mess'. Or:

Donna: "I was very angry, I just went up towards them (the children in the playground). They all ran off except for one. So I shouted at him! I said, 'I heard you call Jo 'Fatface'. I'm angry about it, and I don't want to hear you say that again.' He ran off, of course. But he and the others left Jo alone for the rest of the week."

In making her request, Donna had a result!

• Make requests clear, simple and direct. For example, 'That is my pencil and I want it back'. Practise direct communication with your family.

SAYING NO

• Practise saying 'no' and really meaning it. Children are very good at picking up 'mixed messages' delivered by adults – for example, when an adult *says* 'no' but inwardly might not be feeling good about it. (Then the adult wonders why saying 'no' is not effective and the child doesn't seem to be adhering to it!)

• Say 'no' firmly. There are many ways of saying 'no'. Sometimes saying it quietly and firmly, with eye contact and body language to match, is more effective than a loud, shouted 'no'.

• Practise a range of 'no's, from whispered, to very, very LOUD. Try turning it into a game! The more you and your child practise, the more confident you will become.

Like the other skills, the more effective you become in saying 'no', the more your child will learn:
a) it's all right to say 'no' and,
b) how to say 'no' and really mean it.

This will stand her or him in good stead in all sorts of situations. Remind your child she/he has the right to say 'no' if they want to.

• Warning: be prepared to allow your child to practise saying no to you sometimes!

RESPONDING TO REQUESTS

If someone makes a request and you're not sure if you can agree to it or not, say, 'I'm not sure'. Say you need time to think about it. Teenagers especially, may be under pressure from their peer group to do something they don't really want to do. Help children, from an early age, feel empowered to make their own choices.

If the answer to a request is 'no', it can be useful to be able to suggest an alternative: for example, 'No, I don't want to go to the park. Let's play in the sandpit instead.' It's also everybody's right to be able to change their mind.

It's important to convey to our children that, when we say 'no' to someone, we are not rejecting the person, only refusing the request. If the other person has strong feelings about that, that is their problem. (There may then need to be further negotiations to work out a compromise, though it very much depends on the situation. Some situations are not negotiable.)

SETTING BOUNDARIES

Saying 'no', and making assertive statements are all useful and effective ways of setting boundaries. If your child has been bullied, she/he may need help in redefining and strengthening her or his personal boundaries. Bullying is a violation of boundaries.

If your child has been bullying others, she or he will need firm boundaries set in order to stop the bullying behaviour. You will need to be competently assertive as well as supportive.

Setting boundaries is not so much a skill as an art in itself. It is knowing when to be giving and when to stand firm. It is an integral part of working out discipline with our children. In the way that the river banks are the boundary for a river, holding the river in place whilst still allowing it the freedom to flow, so do we, as parents, help to provide secure boundaries for our children whilst enabling them to grow and flow through different ages and stages of development.

If you would like help with setting boundaries, or with any of the skills (and more!) mentioned in this chapter, you might want to consider assertiveness and/or parenting classes. (See Useful Addresses at the end of the book; also check your local library or adult education college for details of what's available in your area.) Classes offer support and opportunities to put the theory into practice – which, unfortunately, it is not possible to do in a book!

Chapter Six
STAYING SAFE

To equip our children to stay safe, it's important to give them strategies for self-protection. This will help them deal with difficult situations and avoid bullying in the future.

Knowing how to stay safe is also an *attitude*. As parents, it can be difficult, at times, finding the balance between protecting our children and allowing them freedom to develop their independence. We need to alert them to dangers while also helping them develop confidence in themselves and trust (generally) in the world.

If we are very fearful and over-protective towards our children, we may instil a fearful attitude in them. A fearful attitude is more likely to attract bullying. It is more helpful if we nurture a positive attitude in a child, where she/he is aware of the risks, and knows how to respond (which includes running away and seeking help if necessary). In the same way that we help our children learn road sense, we do them as much a service enabling them to be a bit 'street wise' as well – that is, being alert and able to assess ('suss') people and situations.

You and your child, or teenager, might like to practise some of the following strategies in role play situations. Some of them specifically address teenagers and older children so that they can take them away and read them. (Adapt as necessary.)

STRATEGIES FOR SELF-PROTECTION

• Stick with friends whenever possible when in the playground or when there are bullies around. Try to avoid being in 'danger spots' on your own (e.g. toilets, corridors). Stay within sight of a teacher or supervisor.

• Avoid taking valuable possessions to school or wearing expensive jewellery or clothing. Avoid 'showing off' about possessions. If you are threatened with violence to get money or possessions, it's better to give them up than be hurt in a fight. Your safety is more important! Tell a trusted adult as soon as possible about what happened and who was involved.

Talk through how you can prevent it happening again.

• Avoid being provoked into a fight. Bullying behaviour is often physical, and bullies might intentionally pick a fight with someone they can easily beat. (Especially if they're showing off to an audience.) Your safety is more important than their pride. There might be onlookers jeering and taunting, calling you a coward. Ignore them. It takes strength and courage to walk away.

• Stay cool even if insulted. That doesn't mean you *agree* with the insult. Practise saying 'no' and walking away. Or you could make an assertive response, such as, 'No, I'm not smelly, *and* I don't want to fight,' or you could refute name-calling, such as, 'Yes, I come from India/Africa/Outer Mongolia – so what?' WALK AWAY and seek help if necessary. (Racial bullying and other forms of harrassment must be reported.)

• Be aware of, and resist attempts to manipulate you into being upset. Bullies often provoke *in order to* get a reaction. Becoming upset only encourages them. If your response is clear and neutral, showing they're *not* 'getting' to you, they may leave you alone. (Even if they are 'getting' to you, learn to hide it! Then express your feelings about it later, when you are safe at home.)

• Sometimes a show of inner strength is as effective a way to stand up to a bully as a show of physical strength. This may just be a *look* that says 'don't mess with me'. This happens in the adult world as well as with children:

Jim: "Sometimes, in the pub, a bloke will goad you, poke you to provoke a response. He might say, 'Come on then,' trying to pick a fight. But the thing is <u>not</u> *to get goaded, to stand there and take it and hold your ground. Make it clear that if he did anything else you* <u>wouldn't</u> *stand it. You learn to stand your ground, not giving in but not pushing back either. It's quite subtle, quite an art really. It's a lot to do with your expression, and body language. It's taken me many rough situations, years of practice! to learn it. It's something to do with accessing, or exercising your inner strength..."*

• Be aware of posture and body language. Learn to be able to stand up a bit more straightly and to be able to look someone in the eye.

• Even if you've managed to get out of a threatening situation without having to fight, tell someone you trust about it afterwards. It will probably help you to talk about it. You may feel shaken up, or angry or humiliated because you were insulted. Appreciate yourself for handling a difficult situation – remember, it's not the movies! You don't have to be 'heroic'...

• If someone threatens to hurt you, threaten to tell. Make sure you do tell an adult (a teacher, or a playground supervisor for example). This shows you mean business. It also helps to protect you from violence. Your safety is more important than the risk of being called a 'tell-tale'. You are asking for help, not telling tales.

• Learn physical self-defence. This is not suggesting you engage in fights. But having the skills can increase your confidence and belief in your own strength, as well as the ability to get out of threatening situations.

Ali: "After the self-defence classes I learned to respond quickly and knew I had strength, knew I could shout or kick if I had to."

If you have been a bully, self-defence classes might help you use your anger and aggression and fighting skills in a more positive way. (See your local library for details.)

• Learn 'breakaway' techniques. These are different from self-defence techniques in that they are designed to help you escape if attacked or physically restrained. They are taught in some self-defence classes, or 'breakaway' classes run by community groups. (See local library for details.)

• Trust your intuition. Listen to your body and to your feelings: feelings give us a great deal of information. Most of us can remember a time when we sensed risk or danger, and our senses were accurate. Learn to 'tune in' and respond early to any signs. This is something you could practise with your family – not just about danger, but about other things going on. You could turn it into a game: 'I have a feeling that...' and test for accuracy!

• Keep your distance from a bully, or bullying group, wherever possible. Imagine the bully as a magnet, with a strong energy field. How big is the energy field? (Try pacing it out when you're at home, away from the bullying situation. Then measure your own.)

• Work at strengthening, and protecting your own energy field. Some counsellors, for example, visualise themselves sealed in a big blue bubble, to keep their energy field separate from their client's. This is known as psychic protection. Others visualise themselves surrounded in light; others pray for protection.

• Break the rules. We have to give our children permission to 'break the rules' sometimes, if their safety is at risk. Even young children learn early on that they have to always 'be polite' and 'never tell lies'etc. But it's very important to tell our children that, in a crisis, it's okay to break the rules, and break away from the situation in whatever way they like!

This may mean lying – saying, 'The teacher's coming here in a minute' – or kicking or biting to get away, or shouting or swearing or screaming. The purpose is to get away quickly and seek adult help.

Donna: "We have a no-smacking policy in our household, and have always encouraged our children never to hit anyone or to hit back. But we've also told them to hit if they have to! If their safety or survival depends on it."

• Learn to shout. It's good to shout! Practise having a good shout next time you're in a wide open space. Just knowing you're capable of it can help you feel more confident, knowing it's another resource at your disposal. Again, your safety may depend on it.

Greta: "Once, when I was attacked on my bike, I shouted, and ripped the sleeve of my attacker. He ran away. The shouting seemed to give me strength and, of course, drew the attention of other people. I don't really like to shout, but it gives me strength knowing I can if I really need to..."

• Use your anger. Again, sometimes we need permission to feel able to express our anger. But anger is power, and can give us great strength if we use it wisely. If we get angry and upset, that may make bullying worse. But if we calmly channel our anger into power, we may have more effect in a crisis than 'freezing' in fear.

Kate: "When I was fourteen, I was with a younger boy one day out on our bikes. We were cycling home, and had to cross a bridge over a stream. On the other side, were three older boys waving a big stick or an iron bar or something. So, I put my bike down and marched up to them, grabbed the stick and waved it around. I hit one of them on the head, accidentally. He was reeling and they all backed down, let us through. I was shattered, shocked! and still looking over my shoulder to see if the one who had been hit wasn't too badly hurt. But most of all I was furious: the fact that these so-called strong boys had backed down made me realise they weren't seriously threatening us – to them, it was just a bit of fun. But to us it was survival, we had to get home. I hadn't really stopped to think about it, just saw red and did what had to be done. I suppose it was a case of 'fight' or 'flight', and I fought!"

• Make sure you are accompanied (either by an adult or other children) if taking a new route – whether walking or travelling on public transport. Check out any 'risk' spots or difficult parts of the journey. Continue to be accompanied until you are confident and familiar with the route. If at any time the route seems unsafe, or you feel insecure, always ask to be accompanied. (Even if you know your parent is unavailable that time of day, she or he might be able to arrange for someone else to travel with you.)

• If you are old enough, always have a phonecard or money to use a phone in case of emergency (for example to or from school). 999 calls are free. The police have a duty to protect you. Memorise the phone number of your parents and a daytime number where you can contact them, or the adult responsible for your well-being.

• Call helplines such as Childline for advice and counselling on bullying (including if you are someone who is attempting to give up bullying behaviour). If you are at boarding school and it is difficult to make phonecalls in private, talk to a sympathetic teacher. Or, you could write to your parents or Childline. (Be sure to put your address so they can reply to you.)

• Be aware of group dynamics.

Being bullied by a gang, or a group of people can be deeply distressing, especially if your friends are amongst those taking part or watching. Sometimes, because of group dynamics, people do things they might not do on their own. It is good to be aware of the dangers of group/gang psychology so that you can recognise it and avoid falling victim to it. A group can become like a big entity with a life of its own; in this situation, it may not be possible to get sense out of individuals.

As a member of a group or gang, learn to avoid being pressurised to do unkind or cruel things you wouldn't normally do. Even if you're standing not doing anything, just by being an onlooker you may be encouraging the behaviour. You and others may be scared to say anything, in case *you* get bullied.

But then, if you're feeling like that, the chances are that others may be feeling the same as you.

You could try appealing to the better nature of some

of the people in the group to support you in stopping what is happening. If the situation is really out of hand, do not take part, or stand and watch. Leave, if you can, and call for help.

Sometimes, surrendering to the group mentality means individuals can avoid taking responsibility for their actions. They might do something they later regret or feel ashamed of. You can't take responsibility for others' actions. But taking responsibility for your *own* actions may help you, and others, stay safe. It will also help your self-respect.

• Enjoy Group Support.

Not all groups are bullying groups! The advantage of belonging to groups is that there is safety in numbers. Belonging to a 'peer' group can also be a source of strength, enjoyment, mutual learning and support. For adolescents and teenagers, especially, the peer group can play a developmental role in making the transition from being dependent on their parents to becoming independent young adults. For younger children, a group helps develop friendships and social skills. Although parents sometimes find peer groups (especially of teenagers) threatening, because of their influence on their child, it's important to recognise their value. Again, the most important influence *you*, as the parent, can have is to help your child take responsibility for their actions and empower them to make their own decisions (within reason), without being pressurised by others. The home is the best place to practise this! Give your child or teenager the opportunity to make choices and *allow* them to make decisions for themselves. Even when *you* put them under pressure!

• Be aware of the positive power of thought. Even before the fist, the most powerful aspect of bullying behaviour is the bully's psyche, making the victim (or victim-to-be) feel inferior, inadequate and intimidated. One of the ways we can prevent ourselves from giving power to the bully's thoughts, is to create and strengthen our own thoughts about ourselves. For example, to practise saying 'affirmations'. Affirmations are positive thoughts that affirm our belief in ourselves – for example, 'I love and approve of myself,' or, 'I am protected and safe.'

Affirmations work best when used regularly and repeated over and over again, for example when on a daily journey, or when going to sleep. They help increase our inner strength and confidence. Try one!

STRATEGIES FOR SELF-MANAGEMENT IF PRONE TO BULLYING BEHAVIOUR

• Think of ways of removing yourself from situations where you get into trouble.

• Learn assertive, rather than aggressive ways of behaviour. Learn how to express your needs without hurting others. (See local library for details of assertiveness classes in your area.)

• Learn to manage your anger so that you can use it as

a constructive, rather than a destructive force.

• Learn to avoid fights or arguments for their own sake.

• Learn to manage your feelings and accept the situation if others disagree with you or if you don't get your own way.

• Learn to ask for help if you need it: if something is troubling you or if you have a personal or family problem.

If there is nobody you feel you can talk to, try ringing Childline or another helpline. (Details are in the back of the book.)

• Learn to talk about your feelings rather than keep them 'bottled up'. This might be hard if no one in your family shares their feelings. Again, it might help to have telephone counselling or to find someone else (a mentor) to talk to.

• Reflect on *why* you bully. Is it to feel powerful? Or to get attention? Think of other ways of meeting those needs.

• Think about what kinds of friendship you would like. Do you enjoy people being afraid of you or respecting you just because you're 'tough'? Generally, real respect and friendship are earned in other ways.

• Observe how relaxed, confident, happy people get

on together without needing to bully or control each other. Are there ways of doing things you can learn from?

• Are you bullied at home – by your parents or brothers or sisters? If so, seek help to have the bullying stopped. (Phone Childline or the NSPCC or talk to a trusted adult.)

• Think how painful it is to be bullied. Think of how you would like to be treated and start trying to treat yourself and others in more positive ways.

• Think about the pain that verbal bullying can cause. Sometimes people don't realise how distressing teasing can be.
Are you aware that teasing is bullying?

• Take up a sport you enjoy. Channel your physical energies and aggression! It's alright to 'beat' others in sport, so long as you stick to the rules of the game. (Decide on a sport you might enjoy and check out your local recreation centre to see what's available.)

• Take up another physical activity, such as skating or dancing.

• Develop your qualities of leadership. It may be that you dominate and control others in a group. Try leading by example instead. (Rule by respect, not fear!) Good leaders are those who look after the members in their group, making sure everyone is treated fairly and everyone's point of view is heard. Perhaps joining an outward bound course (or equivalent) is something that might channel and develop your leadership skills.

• Think about the heroes you admire in films, books or television. Are they heroes who settle all arguments by violence? If so, try to think of other heroes who win through by using other kinds of strength.

• Think about what irritates you in other people. There may be all kinds of reasons for their appearance or their behaviour that you don't even know about. Try to see others as whole people and accept that we are all different anyway.

• Think about alternatives. For example, if you enjoy bullying because you like showing off in front of an audience, try taking up sports or acting. There are ways of performing to an audience without hurting other people.

• Develop your creative abilities. If you like drawing, or music, for example, seek encouragement so that you can develop your talents. This will help you express yourself and feel more 'connected' to yourself and others. Refuse to settle for boredom and frustration!

• Sort out your education. If it's not working for you, say so. Seek help from parents, family friends, youth workers, teachers, school counsellors and school welfare officers. Phone helplines for further advice.

SAFETY IN THE COMMUNITY

Safety is a community, as well as a personal issue. Schools have the responsibility to provide education in a safe environment. Police have a responsibility to ensure that the law is observed to protect the safety of citizens. Most areas have Police Liaison Officers to give advice on safety.

Form networks of support with other parents. Help your child get into good habits of letting you know where they are going and who they are going with. Set an example by doing the same thing yourself.

Make sure your children and teenagers are clear about their right to safety, and know who to turn to if their safety is threatened.

Encourage your children to be community-minded citizens, and to report any bullying or cruelty they witness. Advise them to 'stay safe' and not to put their personal safety at risk.

THINK SAFE

When we're seeing our children out of the door, it may help them if we convey a positive message rather than a fearful one. 'Think safe', or 'keep safe' is more empowering to a child than 'don't get into any fights' or 'don't get hurt!'

In the same way that, if we say to someone 'don't spill it', what generally happens? They spill it! If we say, 'Carry it carefully' or, 'Cross the road safely' we are helping to give the child a positive picture to take with them.

TAKE TIME TO RELATE

One of the reasons for the fragmentation of our families and communities is the way technology and mobility have helped to turn families into self-sufficient units, often with no need to be involved in the rest of the community, or even be involved, very much, with other family members. In our complex society, many individuals experience overload of information and just want to 'switch off' when they are home!

But remember, for all the technological breakthroughs, interpersonal communication is still the way we develop and grow and help our children develop and grow as well. Take time to talk about feelings and to listen to your children, so that they can talk about their feelings as well.

This way you and your children can share any concerns or anxieties, and support one another in helping to stay safe.

Chapter Seven

SOLUTIONS

In conclusion, it takes time and effort to overcome bullying. If you've read this far, you're probably committed to finding solutions, both as a parent and a citizen.

A successful approach to bullying involves schools, parents and the community working together. And, of course, the children.

A. CHILDREN

Nowadays, in society, there is more awareness, recognition and legislation about Children's Rights. Children, too, are becoming more aware of their personal rights, and learning that they have the right to safety, and to seek protection against harmful behaviour.

Children often know what they need, and what they want to happen. If adults sit down to talk, and listen to them, children often come up with their own solutions, or, child and adult may be able to work out solutions to a difficult situation together.

Eilish (parent of Iain, aged 11): "After we talked, we decided it would be best to ask the teacher for help. Iain wanted to handle the situation (being bullied) himself and

<u>didn't</u> *want the teacher to intervene; however, he wanted to feel he had some backup, if necessary. Now he feels more confident to deal with it, knowing he has the teacher's support. What's also interesting, is that the bullying seems to have stopped!"*

Children, like adults, need space to be able to express their feelings, to feel loved and accepted, and to feel supported in what they're going through. (This doesn't mean that parents, or teachers, need to involve themselves in every aspect of a child's life or ask questions all the time – this would be invasive! However, it does mean being available to listen, about triumphs as well as problems, should a child wish to talk.)

The more a child feels supported at home and at school, the more self-confident and secure she or he will feel. This creates conditions in which she or he can flourish and grow, and the need for bullying behaviour is less likely to take hold.

Many of the skills and strategies included in this book help to empower and protect children as individuals. It takes a broader, more comprehensive approach to fully overcome, and prevent bullying.

B. SCHOOL

Schools that have been successful in drastically reducing levels of bullying have generally included staff *and* pupils in finding solutions.

Anti-bullying policies are effective only if they involve all sectors of the school community, from school governors to teachers and pupils, to parents and non-teaching staff (playground supervisors, dinner staff, pastoral staff etc). Involvement includes helping to develop, as well as implementing the policy. Ideally, any anti-bullying policy helps to create a non-bullying culture in the school, and is part of a broader code of discipline that sets clear guidelines as to what is acceptable, and unacceptable behaviour.

AN EFFECTIVE ANTI-BULLYING POLICY

Different schools require different policies to meet their diverse needs. What is important for all of them, however, is that everyone, from staff to pupils, knows what the policy is and how it works. Children and parents need to know what channels they can use to express any concerns they may have, and pupils and staff need to know what is required of them and what procedures to follow in order to prevent or report bullying behaviour, or to ask for support.

Here are some other functions of an anti-bullying policy:

- To raise awareness about bullying issues

- To ensure anti-discriminatory practice

- To monitor behaviour

- To help older pupils help younger ones

- To help motivate peer pressure so that pupils take

an active stand against bullying behaviour (rather than being onlookers)

• To create a safer school environment, including safer, and more 'child-friendly' playgrounds, with adequate supervision

• To help children be more inclusive of one another

• To create a respectful, and co-operative culture in school

• To encourage parents and teachers to co-operate and communicate.

ALTERNATIVES TO PUNISHMENT

There is much evidence to show that a cycle of punishment and control is not a solution to bullying. Punishment tends to lead to more bullying because, after all, bullying itself is a form of punishment and control and domination.

Some schools adopt a 'no-blame' approach to bullying: that is, taking a problem-solving approach, rather than a blameful, and punitive one. The idea is to reach the empathic feelings within individuals in order to help them:

a) realise the effects of their bullying behaviour and
b) take responsibility for changing their behaviour, with the support and understanding of others.

This does not mean being 'soft' with bullies! Victims are always given support, and any bullying behaviour has to be stopped immediately. It means taking clear, firm and cohesive action that involves pupils, teaching staff, non-teaching staff and parents. It is a long-term, and extremely effective approach that requires time, commitment and training. (For further information, see Useful Addresses at the end of the book.)

RESPECTING THE NEEDS OF CHILDREN

In schools where there is a low incidence of bullying, children are treated respectfully and consulted rather than controlled. They are given responsibility for helping to create a code of discipline and, in some cases, for helping to write the rules!

EMOTIONAL SUPPORT

Many primary schools now have Quality Circles, in which children and teacher take time to sit in a circle and speak about their feelings and listen to one another. In other words, children formally receive and give emotional support, and feelings that often cause anti-social behaviour are addressed early on.

More and more people believe that the emotional well-being of children should be an integral part of school life. They see 'emotional literacy' as being as vital to the well-being of society as the '3Rs'. Many believe that 'relational education' should form part of the school curriculum; others are working towards that end.

Many schools already use art and poetry to help children express feelings, or use drama to help them enact and interpret imaginary and real-life situations. Even the use of 'feedback' – enabling children to give and receive honest and constructive criticism about their work or their behaviour – is more useful in helping children to learn than destructive criticism or 'put-downs' that make them feel a failure. In the same way that, say, with a technical error a child can say, 'I've made a mistake', or, 'It isn't working', a child who is allowed to admit a flaw in their behaviour is more likely to feel encouraged to try new ways, especially if she/he feels supported (rather than punished) in doing so.

C. TEACHERS

Teachers, too, need to feel supported in order to give of their best. It is a sad fact that many teachers who excel in their profession feel under-valued, unappreciated and under pressure from the demands of the school curriculum and the pressures, in many schools, of under-funding.

Classroom Management

Large numbers of pupils, combined with low resources, lead to stress in the classroom, for teachers and pupils. More stress tends to lead to more bullying behaviour. It's hard for a teacher to be in the 'driving seat' and able to give attention to individuals at the same time. One way of a teacher receiving help is to work alongside a Classroom Assistant (or 'Learning Assistant', as they are sometimes called). The role of the assistant is to assist the teacher in practical tasks and to give support and encouragement to pupils in their learning. (There is also, obviously, an element of moral support for the teacher!)

Training

Many teachers, and supervisors, have received little, or no training in behaviour management or group dynamics or assertiveness or, indeed, in communication skills. Many would benefit from learning respectful and effective ways of dealing openly with aggressive and anti-social behaviour. It might also help them to learn effective methods of discipline and ways of enlisting co-operation in their pupils.

Sometimes teachers also need to be made aware of the effects of bullying in children so that they understand, and empathise with the victims.

Welcoming Diversity

Many teachers undergo training to help them overcome discrimination and prejudice in school. Teachers have a major role to play in helping children understand differences in race, culture, religion, ability and needs.

Own Behaviour

A bullying teacher who bullies a class validates bullying in the school. Teachers need to be encouraged, sometimes, to look at their own behaviour, both in the classroom and the staff room, and to assess whether there might not be 'room for improvement...'

Nurturing

Above all, teachers themselves need quality time in which they feel supported and nourished, in order to be able to provide a supportive and nurturing learning environment for their pupils.

D. PARENTS

'A parent's job is terrible hard...'

Parents, too, need to feel supported and valued in the complex and highly demanding task of parenting. Many parents appear to be confident but, when asked, express a whole range of anxieties, guilt, self-doubt and lack of confidence in their abilities.

In order to help our children develop self-esteem and confidence, *we* need to be able to feel self-esteem and confidence in ourselves. Here are some suggestions for parents (for further information see Useful Addresses at the end of the book):

• Give up trying to be 'perfect'. If we expect too much of ourselves we will set ourselves up to fail, feel inadequate and believe that we have somehow 'fallen short' of the mark.

• Appreciate what you do *well* as a parent. Think of something *right now*. It could be anything, from 'reading the children a bedtime story' to 'this morning I comforted Hannah when she was crying'.

• Develop the *habit* of giving yourself (and your partner, if you have one) appreciation and *constructive*, rather than negative criticism.

• Learn from your 'mistakes' and experiences rather than punish yourself for them. For example, 'OK, so I ranted and raved at the kids today. What could I do if the same thing happened tomorrow?' Think of some tactics that could help you (and them). This is also a useful way of helping children accept *their* mistakes and learn from them.

• Join a parenting class, to learn new strategies and develop your skills. It can be easier to feel supported and encouraged in a group rather than struggle trying to make changes on your own. Discussing issues with other parents and having tuition in assertiveness and communication skills can benefit both you and your children. (Children generally *like* the idea of Mummy or Daddy going to a class on parenting!)

• Heal the Past. You may have painful memories of bullying from your own childhood. If so, it is never too late to seek help, break the silence and speak out. That way, as well as helping yourself, you will be more available to help your children than if bullying is such a painful issue for you that you can hardly talk about it. It may help you to talk to a professional therapist or counsellor.

• Handle your own issues. In other words, if you feel an excessive amount of fear, for example, it might be more helpful, for you and your children, if you explore what is making *you* fearful, and where the fear comes from, rather than instilling fear in them. Or, if you have over-high expectations of your children, you may be expressing your own unfulfilled ambition. Again, it may help to talk to a professional therapist or counsellor.

• Accept differences. Use work, friends and acquaintances, education or groups as an opportunity to learn to understand differences in values, or race, or religion, or gender, or sexuality, or culture. We need to free ourselves of our own prejudices in order to help promote understanding in our children.

Susannah (New Age Traveller): "When we went to schools we were bullied because other children's <u>parents</u> told them not to speak or play with us..."

• Respect your own needs. Often, as parents, our own needs become subsumed in meeting the many needs of our children. But our needs are important too! If we make sure we meet some, even if not all, of our needs, it makes us more pleasant, relaxed and less stressed as a person!

• Respect yourself as a person. Allow yourself to feel

vulnerable and to listen to your feelings. Give yourself permission to fail, make mistakes and to feel needy sometimes. It's alright to admit to needing parenting yourself, sometimes.

E. COMMUNITY

Overcoming bullying in the community, again, needs a cohesive approach between schools, youth workers, parents and police. There have been many successful projects, often initiated by schools, where representatives from different schools and different sectors of the community (including shopkeepers and bus drivers, who transport children to and from school) have joined in discussing issues, forming plans and taking action.

Many authorities are recognising the need to have large-scale, community-based programmes in crime prevention (including bullying). One of the most effective ways to keep children, and other citizens, safe is to help build relationships within the community and to help strengthen the community itself.

Mediation services, too, play an important role in community-building by facilitating conflict resolution and in helping members of the community to accept differences. (See Useful Addresses at the end of the book.)

F. Global Community

Earlier, we looked at how bullying behaviour can be a symptom that a child may have a problem. In the same way, in areas where there is a high incidence of bullying, the bullying behaviour is often a symptom of all kinds of problems – not just personal but societal.

It seems no coincidence that, in schools where there is no emotional support, or where emotions are denied, there is a greater risk of physical bullying. Neither does it seem a coincidence that, in areas where there is high unemployment, inadequate housing, poverty and poor health, schools have a higher incidence of bullying and other forms of disruptive behaviour.

One of the solutions, therefore, in overcoming bullying, is for politicians and government to recognise some of the causes of anti-social behaviour and to help under-resourced communities get their needs met. Poverty is one of the world's greatest problems.

Another world problem is war. Large countries bully smaller countries, and differences between countries are perpetuated by attitudes of 'us' and 'them'. You may not feel able to do much for world peace, but you, and your child, might be able to adopt an attitude that is more accepting of everyone's differences. And, if you have succeeded in helping your child overcome bullying, at least you are preventing him or her from experiencing school, or the community, as a war-zone.

APPENDIX

USEFUL ADDRESSES AND RESOURCES

1. Advisory Centre for Education (ACE)
   22 Highbury Grove
   London N5 2DQ
   Tel: 0171-354 8321
   Advice and information on education

2. Anti-bullying Campaign
   10 Borough High Street
   London SE1 9QQ
   Helpline: 0171-378 1446
   Helping parents work with schools to combat the problem
   of bullying. Helps set up Anti-bullying policies.

3. Antidote
   13 Streatley Road
   London NW6 7LJ
   Tel: 0171-328 3284
   Promoting emotional literacy

4. British Association of Counselling
Tel: 01788 578328
Information line for details of local counsellors

5. British Dyslexia Association
98 London Road
Reading
Berkshire RG1 5AU
Helpline: 01734 668271

6. *Bullying: Don't Suffer In Silence. An Anti-bullying pack for Schools (1994)* based on the outcomes of the DEF (Department of Education)-funded Sheffield University anti-bullying project.
HMSO Publications
PO Box 276
London SW8 5DT
Tel. orders: 0171-873 9090

7. *Catering for Children with 'Special Educational Needs'*
Newham Conflict and Change Project
Christopher House
2A Streatfield Avenue
East Ham
London E6 2LA
Tel: 0181-552 2050

8. Childline
   Tel: 0800 1111 or write (remembering to put own address) to:
   Freepost 1111
   London N1 OBR
   A confidential 24-hour phone line for children in trouble or danger.

9. The Children's Legal Centre
   University of Essex
   Wivenhoe Park
   Colchester CO4 3SQ
   Advice line: 01206 873820

10. Commission for Racial Equality (CRE)
    Elliot House
    10-12 Allington Street
    London SW1E 5HE
    Tel: 0171-828 7022

11. Contact-A-Family
    170 Tottenham Court Road
    London W1P 0HA
    Helpline: 0171-383 3555
    Information and support for parents of children with disabilities.

12. Cruse Bereavement Care
Cruse House
126 Sheen Road
Richmond
Surrey TW9 1UE
Bereavement line: 0181-332 7227

13. *Don't Pick on Me - How to Handle Bullying*
by Rosemary Stones
Piccadilly Press (1993)
5 Castle Road
London NW1 8PR
Tel: 0171-267 4492

14. Education Otherwise
PO Box 7420
London N9 9SG
Tel: 0891 518303
Advice and information on education at home

15. Families Need Fathers
134 Curtain Road
London EC2A 3AR
Tel: 0171-613 5060
Helpline: 0181-886 0970
*Offers advice, support and representation to parents
(particularly non-custodials) in maintaining a sound
parent/child relationship in divorce/separation.*

16. Gingerbread
National organisation for lone parents.
England Adviceline: 0171-336 8183
Scotland Adviceline: 0141 353 0953
Northern Ireland Adviceline: 01232 234568
Wales Adviceline: 01792 648728

17. Institute of Personnel and Development
IPD House
Camp Road
London SW19 4UX
Survey on Bullying at Work (Nov. 1996)

18. Kidscape
152 Buckingham Palace Road
London SW1W 9TR
Tel: 0171-730 3300
Advice, training programmes and free publications about bullying.

19. Kingston Friends Workshop Group
Quakers Meeting House
78 Eden Street
Kingston Upon Thames
Surrey KT1 1DJ
Tel: 0181-547 1197
Workshops for families and schools coping with abusive or aggressive behaviour

20. Mediation UK
82a Gloucester Road
Bishopston
Bristol BS7 8BN
Tel: 0117 924 1234
The national organisation for mediation in the community.

21. MIND (National Association for Mental Health)
Granta House
15-19 Broadway
London E15 4BQ
Information Line: 0181-522 1728
Advice and free publications on mental health. (See also: Young Minds)

22. National Association for the Gifted Child,
Tel: 01908 698498 or 01908 673677.
Taking into account the needs of gifted children.

23. National Coalition Building Institute (NCBI)
PO 411
Leicester LE4 8ZY
Tel: 0116 260 3232
Workshops on Ending Bullying in Schools, Conflict Resolution and Prejudice Reduction.

24. 'The No-blame Approach'
Lucky Duck Enterprises
34 Wellington Park
Clifton
Bristol BS8 2UW
Tel: 0117 973 2881
Training courses and publications on the No-blame approach to bullying.

25. NSPCC (National Society for the Prevention of Cruelty to Children)
42 Curtain Road
London EC2A 3NH
Child Protection Helpline: 0800 800500 (24 hours)
Call this number for advice if you think a child is being harmed.

26. Parentline
Endway House
The Endway
Benfleet
Essex SS7 2AN
Helpline: 01702 559900
Telephone counselling service for parents.

27. Parent Network
Room 2, Winchester House
Kennington Park
11 Cranmore Road
London SW9 1EJ
Tel: 0171-735 1214
Courses enhancing communication and
relationships between parents and children,
for parents in England, Scotland and Wales.

28. Quindo
The Quindo Centre
2 West Drive
London NW11 7QH
Tel: 0181-455 8698
Confidence-building and anti-bullying fitness programme.

29. Relate
Herbert Gray College
Little Church Street
Rugby
Warwickshire CV21 3AP
Tel: 01788 573241
Leading agency for relationship counselling.

30. The Samaritans
Head Office
The Grove
Slough   SL1 1QP
For local helpline numbers look inside the front
cover of your local phone directory.
Confidential telephone support, 24 hours a day,
to suicidal or despairing people.

31. The Sports Council
Information Centre
16 Upper Woburn Place
London WC1H OQP
Tel: 0171-388 1277

32. *Tackling Bullying: Schools, Parents and the*
Community Working Together (1996)
CEDC Publications (Community Education
Development Centre)
Lyng Hall, Blackberry Lane
Coventry CV2 3JS
Tel: 01203 638660

33. Trust for the Study of Adolescence
Tel: 01273 693311
Advice and publications for parents and adolescents.

34. Young Minds
2nd Floor
102-108 Clerkenwell Road
London EC1V 2NP
Tel: 0171-251 3123
Youth Access (provides names of local youth
counsellors): 01509 210420
*Promoting the mental health of children, young
people and their families.*

35. *You Can Heal Your Life* by Louise L. Hay (1984)
Eden Grove Editions
26 Eden Grove
London N7 8EF
*Book containing exercises in self-worth and healing
affirmations.*

INDEX

OTHER BOOKS IN THE *HOW TO HELP YOUR CHILD* SERIES PUBLISHED BY PICCADILLY PRESS

ARE YOU EXPECTING TOO MUCH FROM YOUR CHILD? by Dr Fiona Subotsky
'*...offers a fresh perspective for anyone having a hard time with their kids...uses case studies to show how parents of, say, a crying baby or a bolshy toddler are often worrying about behaviour that is, in fact, developmentally appropriate*' – Time Out

GRAMMAR FOR PARENTS
by Jerry George with Clare Stuart
'*A short but packed with information practical guide to English grammar. An extremely useful book for parents*'
– School Librarian

IT FOR PARENTS
by Adrian and Rosemary Russell
'*The writers communicate their confidence in the intelligence and worth of the reader and impart the required knowledge as if to a valued friend. This little book should grace parents' association stalls across the country. Anyone will benefit from the Russells' down-to-earth informativeness*' – Times Educational Supplement

MATHS FOR PARENTS
by Rosemary Russell
'*...gives excellent support to parents defeated by modern teaching methods and National Curriculum demands*'
– Times Educational Supplement

READING FOR PARENTS
by Irene Yates
'...an easily digested publication of use to anyone with a child learning to read...particularly helpful for parents of reluctant readers' – Time Out

SPELLING FOR PARENTS
by Doreen Scott-Dunne
'...offers refreshingly easy strategies for parents to use with children encountering difficulties with spelling...An optimistic book which should also be useful to adults with spelling difficulties' – Independent

WELL DONE
by Ken Adams
'Adams is particularly good at explaining maths concepts and has lots of useful strategies to impart...good value' – Time Out

WRITING SKILLS FOR PARENTS
by Irene Yates
'Irene Yates writes in a lucid style and this book is useful as much for its accessible information about how children learn as for the suggestions for enjoyable practical projects...manages to be child-, parent- and teacher-friendly simultaneously' – Time Out

CHILD SAFETY FOR PARENTS
by Dr Bill Gillham
This invaluable book gives new insights and essential advice to parents about *effective* ways of protecting their children.